T0151863

THE MIDDLE BRONZE AGE IIA
CEMETERY AT GESHER

THE ANNUAL OF
THE AMERICAN SCHOOLS OF ORIENTAL RESEARCH

Volume 62

Series Editor
Nancy Serwint

THE MIDDLE BRONZE AGE IIA CEMETERY AT GESHER: FINAL REPORT

edited by

Yosef Garfinkel and Susan Cohen

American Schools of Oriental Research • Boston, MA

ANNUAL OF THE AMERICAN SCHOOLS OF ORIENTAL RESEARCH
VOLUME 62

© American Schools of Oriental Research 2007

ISBN: 978-0-89757-075-6

Library of Congress Cataloging-in-Publication Data

The middle Bronze Age IIA cemetery at Gesher : final report /
   edited by Yosef Garfinkel and Susan Cohen.
   p. cm. -- (The annual of the American Schools of Oriental
   Research ; v. 62)
Includes bibliographical references.
ISBN 978-0-89757-075-6 (alk. paper)
1. Gesher Site (Israel) 2. Excavations (Archaeology)--
   Israel--Gesher Site. 3. Bronze age--Israel. 4. Israel-
   -Antiquities. 5. Cemeteries--Israel--Gesher Site. I.
   Garfinkel, Yosef. II. Cohen, Susan.

DS110.G47M53 2007
933--dc22

                              2007039884

Printed in the United States of America on acid-free paper

To
SEYMOUR GITIN

Contents

ILLUSTRATIONS

Tables

Preface

This volume presents the final results of the five seasons of excavation (1986–1987, 2002–2004) at the site of Gesher, a small Middle Bronze Age IIA cemetery located on the eastern slope of the river terrace in the central Jordan Valley in Israel. The site was first discovered in the mid-1970s following Israeli Army activities in the area; during the process of cutting a road on the slope of the hill, archaeological remains from both the Middle Bronze Age and the Pre-Pottery Neolithic A period were exposed and damaged. Subsequent looting of various ceramics and bronze objects dating to the Middle Bronze Age, as well as Neolithic flint and stone artifacts, drew attention to the site.

Gesher was first excavated in 1986–1987 by Dr. Yosef Garfinkel on behalf of the Institute of Archaeology of the Hebrew University of Jerusalem. In those two seasons, in addition to his interests in the Neolithic remains at the site, Garfinkel excavated fifteen burials. Each burial consisted of a single primary interment and numerous grave goods, including ceramics, weapons, and other metals, and faunal remains, were excavated in relation to these individuals. A further three seasons of excavations were then conducted at Gesher by Dr. Susan L. Cohen in 2002–2004 on behalf of Montana State University at Bozeman, Montana. These additional seasons uncovered eight more interments in the cemetery, along with the accompanying grave goods, including ceramic vessels, faunal remains, and three bronze spearheads.

Significantly, however, while all of the material culture from Gesher is clearly typologically consistent with a very early MB IIA date, it also proves to have significant differences from that commonly found at larger urban sites in the more central regions of Canaan. At the same time, many of the burial customs evident in the cemetery show continuities with practices more commonly associated with the preceding EB IV/MB I period. To date, Gesher represents one of the very few sites in Canaan where this transitional phase of development has been identified; further, the corpus of material from Gesher consists almost entirely of whole vessels, as well as metal weapons, in which the transitional nature of the artifacts can be easily identified. This volume outlines the nature of the finds from the cemetery and highlights the information regarding Canaanite mortuary customs and material culture gained from the excavation of this small but significant site.

Acknowledgments

The excavations at Gesher in 1986–1987 were made possible due to funds from the Israel National Council for Research and Development at the Israeli Ministry of Science. The Dorot Foundation and the Philip and Muriel Berman Center for Biblical Archaeology of the Institute of Archaeology at The Hebrew University of Jerusalem supported the final stages of the analysis and its preparation for publication. The pottery was drawn by Mika Sarig and the artifacts were photographed by Gabi Laron.

The small expedition included Dani Nadel as staff member and students of archaeology who participated for various weeks: Angela Davidzon, Rivka Rabinovich, Hannah Greenberg and Absalom Jacobi, as well as numerous volunteers from Israel and abroad, with about 10–15 present at any given time. Room and board were supplied by the nearby Kibbutz Neve Ur, where we enjoyed the warm hospitality of Israel Reich. Technical assistance was provided by Yossi Morag, a geologist from nearby Kibbutz Gesher Gypsum Quarry.

The 2002–2004 excavations at Gesher were made possible through financial support provided by the Office of the Vice President for Research and Creativity and the College of Letters and Science at Montana State University and the ASOR Torch Fund/Harris Grant, in association with ASOR and the Israel Exploration Society. The Dorot Foundation provided financial assistance for student workers in the 2004 season. Room and board was supplied by Kibbutz Shaʿar ha-Golan, and tools and equipment were generously supplied in 2002 by Dr. Y. Garfinkel and the Shaʿar ha-Golan excavations, and in 2003–2004 by Professor L. E. Stager and the Leon Levy Expedition to Ashkelon.

A publications grant from the Archaeological Institute of America provided the funding for the preparation of the material for final publication. The pottery was restored by Moshe Ben-Ari, ceramic drawings were prepared by Mgr. W. Więckowski; the spearhead drawings were rendered by J. Rudman. The objects were photographed by Z. Radovan; maps were prepared by D. Martin and J. Rosenberg; final plates were prepared by R. Evyasaf and J. Rosenberg.

Many thanks are due to Dr. S. Gitin for his advice and assistance in setting up the 2002–2004 excavation and for making available the resources and facilities at the W. F. Albright Institute for Archaeological Research in Jerusalem during work on this publication. Thanks also go to the Council for British Research in the Levant and the Kenyon Institute in Jerusalem, which provided accommodations, work space, and other assistance during the preparation of this manuscript. Prof. R. Rydell from the Department of History and Philosophy at Montana State University provided invaluable administrative support and incredible assistance toward overcoming the many difficulties faced in organizing an archaeological excavation from Bozeman, Montana. And finally, many thanks to J. Baker, O. Cannon, E. Christensen, T. Estrup, D. Phelps, and, last but definitely not least, W. Więckowski; without them, there would have been no excavation.

Chapter 1

Introduction

by Yosef Garfinkel and Susan Cohen

1.1   Site Location and Setting

Gesher is a small site in the central Jordan Valley, about 12 km south of the Sea of Galilee (Lake Kinneret), Israel map reference 202/223 (fig. 1.1), at the intersection of two geographical features: the Nahal Tavor (Wadi Bira), which descends on a west–east line, and the cliff between the upper and lower terraces of the Jordan Valley, which is prominent on a north–south line. The Jordan River flows about 1 km east of the site. The archaeological remains are located to the south of Nahal Tavor on the slope that descends from the upper terrace of the Jordan Valley (Zor) to the lower terrace (Ghor) (fig. 1.2), approximately 242–47 m below sea level. In antiquity, Nahal Tavor would have provided a convenient route towards the west, a variety of plants and animals, and a good source of raw material such as basalt, flint and lime pebbles.

The Jordan River valley is part of a long south–north rift valley from Zimbabwe in Africa to Turkey. It was created by tectonic activity that included both horizontal movement and a vertical sinking of the valley floor. This vertical movement has created steep slopes on both sides of the valley, leaving the river channels as the only convenient routes for human movement to the west and east. Volcanic eruptions covered both the valley floors and the slopes with basaltic cover, and inland lakes have filled the Jordan Valley in various stages.

During part of the last Glacial era (ca. 70,000–15,000 bp), the valley was covered by the Lisan Lake, an inland lake composed of saline water changing from hyper-saline in the south to brackish in the north. After the lake's gradual desiccation, probably before ca. 12,500 bp (Begin et al. 1985), the valley was left covered by sediments that created the Lisan Formation, composed of marls and other evaporates with gravel beds at the tributaries' estuaries. The Jordan River itself, which is a very young river, then started carving its channel in the Lisan sediments. The river created a meandering route and a floodplain 500–1,000 m wide and 30–50 m lower than the valley floor.

The soft Lisan sediment and the active nature of the river's meanders have created a dissected badland. This badland is covered with thick vegetation, rendering almost any approach to the river difficult, thus making its water unexploitable from a human point of view. In contrast, the higher valley floor is relatively flat and was covered in time by fertile alluvium, making it a much more

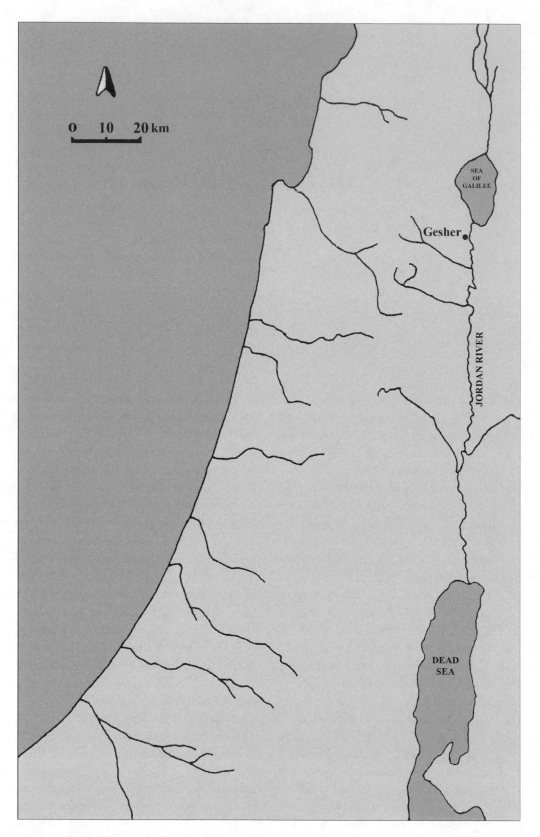

FIG. 1.1   *Map of Canaan showing the location of Gesher.*

FIG. 1.2 *General view of the cliff between the upper and lower terraces of the Jordan Valley and the Gesher excavations, from the north.*

desirable habitat for humans.[1] The low altitude and the mountain ranges to the west create very moderate winters with about 300 mm of annual precipitation and very hot summers with summer average temperature over 30° centigrade and rising to a maximum of well over 40° (Ben-Arieh 1965; Karmon 1971).

1.2   STRATIGRAPHY AND SITE FORMATION PROCESS

Seven layers, geological and anthropological, have been distinguished at the site, numbered here from top to bottom.[2] In the preliminary analysis, the Middle Bronze phase was not assigned a number (Garfinkel and Nadel 1989); in order not to change the sequence already established for the site, the MB IIA phase is marked as Layer 1a in the overall site stratigraphy.

LAYER 1: Light sediment, 2–3 m thick, mostly Lisan in secondary deposition.

LAYER 1A: Middle Bronze IIA tombs cut into the reddish sediment of Layer 2. According to the typology of the various find categories – pottery, bronze weapons, and a toggle pin – the tombs date to the beginning of the early Middle Bronze Age. One radiocarbon measurement, from wood found in association with a bronze axe, yielded the date of ca. 2100–1900 BCE, calibrated (fig. 1.3). Tectonic activities tilted and removed the Neolithic remains; the Middle Bronze Age tombs were undisturbed, however. This clearly indicates that the tectonic events at the site occurred prior to ca. 1950 BCE.

LAYER 2: Reddish sediment, 1–1.5 m thick, mostly homogeneous clay devoid of stones.

LAYER 3: An orange-colored sediment, 20–60 cm thick, including fallen mudbricks, charcoal, bones, and stone and flint artifacts. This layer represents the accumulation of Pre-Pottery Neolithic A occupation debris deposited on the *in situ* Neolithic horizon of Layer 4. This layer, and all the layers beneath it, were disturbed by landslides.

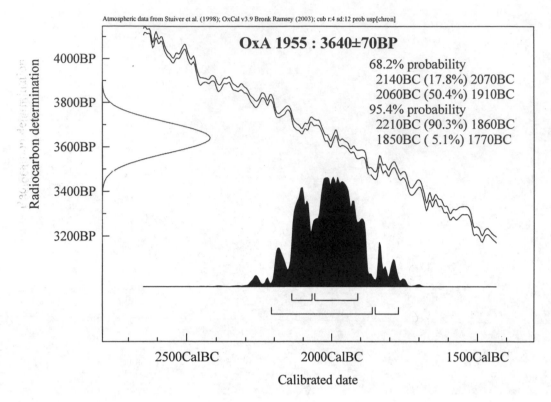

Atmospheric data from Stuiver et al. (1998); OxCal v3.9 Bronk Ramsey (2003); cub r:4 sd:12 prob usp[chron]

OxA 1955 : 3640±70BP

68.2% probability
2140BC (17.8%) 2070BC
2060BC (50.4%) 1910BC
95.4% probability
2210BC (90.3%) 1860BC
1850BC (5.1%) 1770BC

Radiocarbon determination

4000BP
3800BP
3600BP
3400BP
3200BP

2500CalBC   2000CalBC   1500CalBC

Calibrated date

FIG. 1.3   *Calibration curve of the radiometric date from Gesher.*

LAYER 4: A Pre-Pottery Neolithic A settlement, which was dated by four C[14] measurements to ca. 10,000 BCE.[3] Neolithic remains were found in only two sections of the site, Area A and Area B, located approximately 20 m apart. The better preserved Area B included part of a round house with a wall built of massive elongated mudbricks, 40–50 cm long and about 20 cm wide (fig. 1.4). The bricks are plano-convex in section. No stone foundation was found, and the bricks were placed directly on the living floor level. Inside the house, near the wall, there was a hearth, built of small lime pebbles, about 50 cm in diameter, with a rounded concentration of ash adjacent to it. Near the hearth was a large basalt block, about 40 × 50 cm, with a cupmark. A pit containing several ground stone tools was also exposed inside the building. A wealth of small artifacts was collected from the building's floor, including flints, bone tools, basalt tools, a lunate coated with ocher, and ocher lumps; a group of fourteen clay beads was also found on the house floor. Numerous finds were uncovered in the area outside the building to the west, including several dozen ground stone tools, waste and raw basalt chunks. Analysis of the finds from this spot demonstrated that it was an activity area for the production of stone tools.

LAYER 5: A whitish calcitic fine sand, 5–30 cm thick, devoid of stones, deposited directly on the Lisan Formation.

LAYER 6: The Lisan Formation.

While Gesher has rather simple depositional processes regarding the archaeological material at the site, its post-depositional processes are very complicated. The relevant aspects are presented here in chronological order:

1. The Neolithic remains at Gesher lay directly on virgin soil. As observed in many deep sections around Gesher, there are no Natufian remains below or near it, which implies that there is

no nearby Natufian source for potential intrusions.

2. The Neolithic site existed only for a very short time. Only one living surface was discovered in each excavation area, and most of the artifacts were found on these living surfaces.

3. The living surfaces were covered by 30–50 cm of debris. This debris includes fallen mudbricks and probably originated from the building superstructure that collapsed over the floors.

4. After the abandonment of the Neolithic settlement, the area remained unoccupied until the Middle Bronze Age IIA, about 6,000 years later.

5. Tectonic effects took place at the site at some point between the Neolithic and the Middle Bronze Age.

6. During the Middle Bronze Age, the area of Gesher was used as a cemetery. The tombs did not damage the Neolithic remains, but occasionally Neolithic artifacts were found in some of the tombs.

7. The location of the site on the hillside exposed the remains to slope erosion, which works faster than on a level plane. As a result, all of the eastern part of the site has been eroded, and how much is missing is not clear.

8. The site was exposed during the construction of a dirt road in the mid-1970s by the Israeli Army as part of the activities along the border with Jordan. This added to the damage caused by the erosion and resulted in the total or partial destruction of some of the Neolithic remains and several of the Middle Bronze Age burials.

1.3   HISTORY OF EXCAVATIONS AT THE SITE

The archaeological remains at Gesher were buried under an accumulation several meters thick that sealed the site; consequently, the site was not discovered in a survey carried out in this region during the 1950s (Tzori 1962). Gesher was first discovered in the mid-1970s after Israeli Army activities in the area. Deep cuts were made on the

FIG. 1.4   *The remains of a Pre-Pottery Neolithic A rounded structure in Area B.*

slope separating the upper and lower terraces of the Jordan Valley and two roads were built; one is a paved road that created a steep scarp at the bottom of the slope of the hill (the lower cut) and the second is an unpaved road that created a second steep scarp near the top of the slope (the upper cut). Archaeological remains from the Middle Bronze Age II and the Pre-Pottery Neolithic A period were damaged and destroyed by these cuts without being noticed.

Following this activity, Middle Bronze Age II remains were recognized by local farmers, and various ceramics and bronze objects were looted. Some of these were collected by Emanuel Eisenberg and brought to the Israel Department of Antiquities and Museums in Jerusalem (today the Israel Antiquities Authority). These artifacts were published in Hebrew (Hess 1990; see Chapter

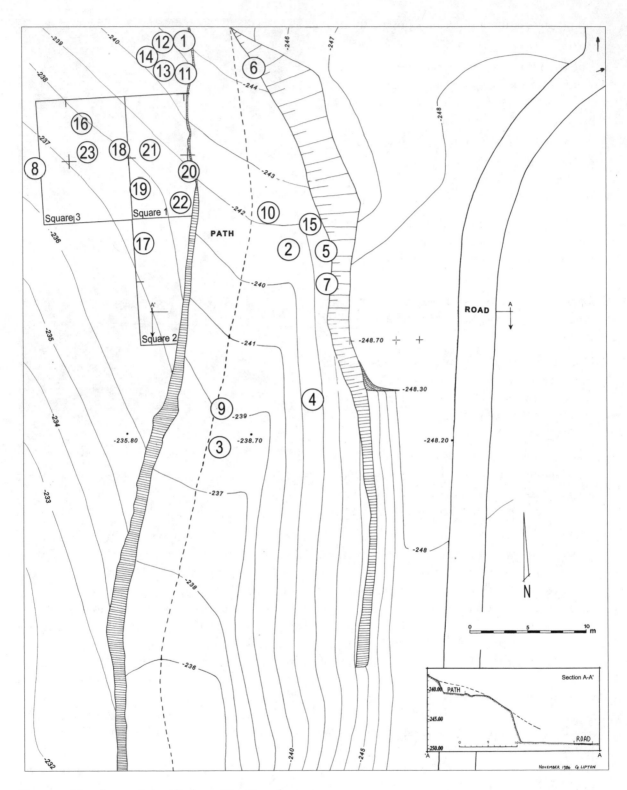

FIG. 1.5 *Map of excavations at Gesher, 1986–1987 and 2002–2004.*

2). Subsequently, it was noticed by Israel Reich of Kibbutz Neve Ur that Neolithic flint and stone artifacts were located in that area as well. This information was brought to the attention of Yosef Garfinkel by Emanuel Eisenberg and Nurit Feig. After a few visits to the site in the mid-1980s, a decision was made to excavate, as there are very few Pre-Pottery Neolithic A sites known in the Levant to date.

Two seasons of excavation were conducted in 1986 and 1987 by Yosef Garfinkel on behalf of the Institute of Archaeology of the Hebrew University of Jerusalem. The first season lasted three weeks during November/December 1986 and concentrated mainly on excavating Area A near the lower cut (Garfinkel 1988). The second season lasted for four weeks during November/December 1987 and concentrated mainly on excavating Area B near the upper cut (Garfinkel 1990a; fig 1.5). The expedition first unearthed a number of Middle Bronze Age IIA graves (Garfinkel 1990b; 1993; 2001; Garfinkel and Bonfil 1990; Maeir and Garfinkel 1992), and further below the Pre-Pottery Neolithic A remains were found (Garfinkel 1990b; 1993; Garfinkel and Nadel 1989; Horwitz and Garfinkel 1991; Garfinkel and Dag 2006).

In the years 2002–2004, three additional excavation seasons were conducted by Susan L. Cohen on behalf of Montana State University at Bozeman, Montana. The first season lasted only ten days and was designed as a preliminary season to examine the possibilities of further excavation in the Middle Bronze Age cemetery (Cohen 2003a). The second season lasted four weeks in June/July 2003, and focused on Square 1, with small exposures in Square 2 to the south and Square 3 to the west (Cohen 2003b; 2004a). The third and final season lasted four weeks in July/August 2004, and expanded the areas excavated in Squares 2 and 3; additionally, Square 1 was excavated to a lower level (Cohen 2004b). The focus of these three seasons was specifically on the Middle Bronze Age remains, and no Neolithic materials were exposed during these excavations.

1.4 Methodology

1.4.1 The 1986–1987 Seasons

Before the start of the excavations, the area was topographically surveyed and a detailed map was created showing heights at intervals of one meter. An absolute height below sea level was established. The various archaeological features were then added onto this map.

At the beginning of the first season, the upper sterile topsoil was removed by tractor. After about 1–3 m the Middle Bronze Age graves started to appear. From this stage on, work was conducted on the site by hand. As the site is located on a cliff, the tractor created a step-like topography, thereby enabling easy access to the excavation areas.

The Middle Bronze Age graves were assigned numbers from 1 to 14 and published (Garfinkel and Bonfil 1990). An additional, badly destroyed, grave was found during a later visit to the site and was assigned the number 15. The skeletons and the various grave goods were systematically uncovered, recorded by photographs and drawings, and then removed. Each artifact received a basket number, and its location and height were marked. All together about 50 such basket numbers were used for the Middle Bronze excavations.

1.4.2 The 2002–2004 Seasons

The later excavations utilized the topographical map first established during the earlier seasons; newer archaeological features were added on this map to show their location in relation to the material excavated previously. These excavations concentrated on the slope above the upper cut; no work was done in the lower areas. Using a fixed point as a benchmark with the absolute value of 250 m below sea level, three areas (Squares 1–3), measuring 10 × 10 m, were laid on the site (fig. 1.5) to establish parameters for excavation. Excavation within each square used sequential locus and bucket numbers, with bucket numbers beginning again at 1 for each new excavation season. Each burial was assigned a number in sequence, resulting in the original designation of Burials 1–8. For compilation of the final excavation report, these numbers have been changed to Graves 16–23 in order to present a synthesized analysis of all the data from the cemetery.[4] In cases of depositions of material culture without associated skeletal remains, each grouping was assigned a separate number from 1–4.

Each burial and deposition was fully exposed, drawn and photographed *in situ*, and then removed. Every ceramic vessel was assigned an individual basket number, and the metal artifacts were recorded with the general bucket associated with each burial. A material culture registration number was also assigned to every object excavated.

1.5.   SIGNIFICANCE OF THE SITE

The site of Gesher has considerable significance for both mortuary and cultural studies of MB IIA development in Canaan. While other MB IIA mortuary sites are often badly disturbed, either by looting in antiquity or through the placement of additional interments in multiple-burial chambers, the graves at Gesher are characterized by undisturbed primary burials found in situ. Although the preservation of the remains, both biological and material, was quite poor (see discussions below in Chapters 3 and 4), the graves preserved the initial deposition of both the skeleton and the associated grave goods with little or no disturbance; thus, it is possible to examine the remains as they were initially deposited and to deduce further information concerning the mortuary practices and customs implemented by the population that utilized the cemetery.

In addition to the undisturbed nature of the site, Gesher is also significant in its early date within the MB IIA cultural horizon. The material culture, although demonstrably of MB IIA type, also shows affinities to the preceding EB IV/MB I period, and, as such, represents one of the few sites in the Levant that provides insight to the transitional period between these two eras. Further, while other sites located in the Jordan Valley region have also produced data regarding this transition, most notably Tell el-Hayyat, these data are limited to sherd evidence only. Because of the undisturbed nature of the Gesher burials, the site has produced more than fifty whole vessels representative of this transitional phase and subsequent early MB IIA development. Gesher's transitional nature is also indicated by the seven "warrior burials" excavated at the site. As a type with origins in the preceding Early Bronze Age period, "warrior burials" have been found at other sites with early MB IIA remains but not in such quantities as those attested at Gesher, where this burial type accounts for almost thirty percent of the excavated portion of the cemetery (see discussion in Chapter 3).

This report presents information regarding the burials, together with discussion regarding each type of material object found in association with the graves, with the goals of providing the information from the cemetery in one complete corpus. This information adds to the data regarding Canaanite mortuary customs and increases the corpus of early MB IIA material culture in connection with trends and customs originating in the preceding era. Gesher provides a window into the transitional period between EB IV / MB I and MB IIA which, to date, is rarely, if ever, attested at other sites, and, consequently, has significant implications for identifying this cultural era in Canaan.

NOTES

1   The alluvium-covering Lisan Formation sediments accumulated mostly after the Neolithic in the immediate vicinity of the site (Belitzky 1996). In addition, the degree of soil salinity decreased through time, as the rainfall washed some of the salts from the Lisan sediments.

2   This complete stratigraphic sequence was observed only in Area A of the 1986–1987 excavations. In Area B, Layers 1 and 5 are missing; the reddish alluvium sediment of Layer 2 is the topsoil there, and the Neolithic remains lie directly on the Lisan. The 2002–2004 excavations

concentrated solely on the Middle Bronze Age cemetery and did not examine this sequence below Layer 2.

3 For a detailed report of the PPNA excavations, see Garfinkel, forthcoming.

4 The interments were cited as Burials 1–8 in all previous publications of the 2002–2004 excavations (Cohen 2003a; 2003b; 2004a; 2004b; 2005). In this final excavation report, Burial 1 is now Grave 16, Burial 2 equals Grave 17, Burial 3 equals Grave 18, and so on, reaching a total of 23 graves from the cemetery as a whole.

Chapter 2

Finds from a Cemetery in Nahal Tavor*

by Orna Hess

This chapter was originally published as an independent article in Hebrew, which presented the material collected from the surface at Gesher, after the site was disturbed by military activities (see Chapter One). For the benefit of the reader, we have chosen to include this article in the final report on the excavations at Gesher, so that all the material recovered from the site is presented together in one volume. The article has been translated directly, without any changes to the original text, except for the figure numbers, which have been altered to be consistent with the sequence of illustrations in this volume, and to change the references to be consistent with the format in use for this volume; all references are listed in full in our bibliography at the end of the volume. It should be noted that we have established our own typology for the ceramics from Gesher that differs from some of the references and parallels discussed here (see Chapter 5).

An MB IIA cemetery was discovered during development works carried out in 1975–1976 and 1978 on the south bank of Nahal Tavor at the point where it drains into the Jordan Valley (map ref. 2023/2231).[1] The tombs, which were dug into the Lisan marl, were apparently arranged in two rows. Around the tombs were large quantities of fired bricks that presumably originated in the Pre-Pottery Neolithic A site. No traces of a contemporary settlement were discerned in the vicinity of the cemetery. Since stratigraphic excavations were not carried out at the site, the finds that were collected will be discussed typologically.

2.1 BOWLS

Five complete bowls were recovered, four of them (fig. 2.1:1–4) of the open, deep type and the fifth (fig. 2.1:5) carinated. The bowls are made of coarse fabric and lack any trace of slip or burnish, although they are generally made with care. The walls and bases are especially thick, making it very likely that these bowls served as everyday vessels.

The bowls in figure 2.1:1–2 have thickened walls that curve inward. Their bases are flat (Loud 1948: pls. 9:4, 14:9; Beck 1975: fig. 6:10). Two additional bowls (fig. 2.1:3–4) have straight walls, flat bases and everted rims. These bowls are very common in the MB IIA (Beck 1975: fig. 4:9; Loud 1948: pl. 9:11; Guy 1938: pl. 31:11; Kochavi et al. 1979: fig. 17:4). Figure 2.1:5 is a small carinated bowl; the carination is somewhat rounded rather than sharp, and the flat base is exceptionally thick (Epstein 1974: fig. 7:7; Loud 1948: pl. 28:34; Kochavi et al. 1979: fig. 7:4).

2.2 JUGLET AND JUGS

Figure 2.1:6, a juglet with a gutter rim and a double handle from the rim to the shoulder, is noteworthy. The juglet, which is red-slipped and burnished,

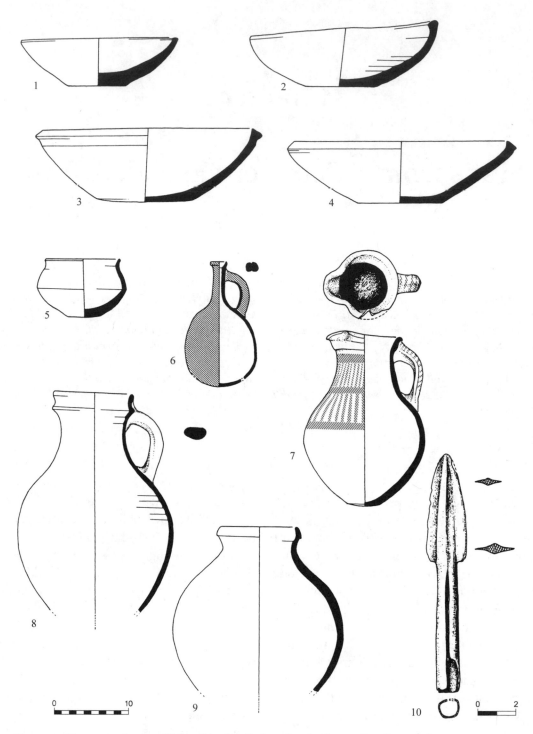

Fig. 2.1 *The group of surface finds collected at Gesher after the site was first discovered.*

has a globular body and a rounded base. The few parallels to this rare type are from Lebea in Lebanon, Munhata, and Megiddo (Guigues 1937: fig. 5:c; Ferembach et al. 1975: fig. 8:1; Loud 1948: pl. 19:31). However, one should point out a similarity in shape between this juglet and decorated juglets from Cyprus, such as one found at Beth Shemesh (Amiran 1969: pl. 37:10), belonging to the Pendant Line Style of White Painted III–IV and dated by Åström to the last phase of the MB IIA (Gerstenblith 1983: 70-72).

Two jugs that are unusual for the period are shown in figure 2.1:7-8. Figure 2.1:7 has an oval, somewhat piriform body and a trefoil rim. Its upper body is painted in red in a pattern consisting of three parallel horizontal lines with vertical lines between them. This pattern is reminiscent of the typical decorative style in the region of Beth Shean and the Jordan Valley in the MB I.[2] Jugs of similar shape were found at Alalakh and in tombs near Sidon (Guigues 1938: fig. 88; Woolley 1955: pl. 85: a), while jugs with a similar decorative motif were found in the same tombs near Sidon and at Ugarit and Tarsus (Guigues 1938: fig. 69; Schaeffer 1949: fig. 108:22). Figure 2.1:8 has a piriform body and a ridge under the rim.[3] This jug type has a long chronological range.[4]

2.3   Jar

A single jar (fig. 2.1:9) was recovered. It has a globular body and gutter rim and lacks handles. Similar jars found in various regions of Palestine are dated to the MB IIA (Loud 1948: pl. 12:16; Ory 1938: 116, nos. 73–74; Tufnell 1962: fig. 12:38.

2.4   Spearhead

The only weapon found in the cemetery is a spearhead with a prominent rib (fig. 2.1:10). This type is common in the MB IIA (Epstein 1974: fig. 14:7; Dunand 1950: pl. 58:82; Pritchard 1963: fig. 64:12).

2.5   Summary

The assemblage displays a number of prominent characteristics:
1. Flat bases that are worked and emphasized are especially typical of the bowls; ring bases are apparently entirely lacking.
2. Only two vessels are slipped or decorated.
3. Most of the vessels are typical of the MB II, particularly its early part. However, it is possible that there was a later phase of use of the site, perhaps represented by the jug in figure 1.8.

The MB IIA cemetery at this site in the Jordan Valley contributes important information, since it is one of the few known sites in the region that are dated to this phase of the MB II.

Notes

* This report was first published in Hebrew in 'Atiqot 10 (1990), 157–59. Translation by Susan M. Gorodetsky.

1 The site was reported by Y. Porath, an inspector of the Israel Department of Antiquities and Museums. The finds presented here were drawn by Michal Ben-Gal. The plate was prepared by Liora Minbitz.

2 For example in the cemetery of 'En ha-Natziv (unpublished) and at Megiddo and el-Hutzan.

3 A similar vessel (No. 509–1789) was found in Tomb 92 in the excavations carried out by Emmanuel Eisenberg at Tel Kitan. I am grateful to the excavator for permitting me to mention this vessel. See also Kenyon 1965: fig. 93:4; Loud 1948: pl. 25:14; Ferembach et al. 1975: fig. 8:10 (from a tomb dated to the MB IIA–B transition).

4 For example, at Lachish a vessel with an identical rim appears in the Late Bronze Age (Tufnell 1958: pl. 75:688).

Chapter 3

The Burials

by Yosef Garfinkel and Susan Cohen

3.1 THE EXCAVATIONS

3.1.1 Introduction

During the 1986–1987 seasons at Gesher, while cleaning overburden sediment and digging towards the Neolithic layers, fourteen Middle Bronze Age IIA graves were located and systematically excavated. The remains of another grave, No. 15, were collected at a later stage, after the site was damaged by a local farmer. In 2002–2004 excavations were resumed at Gesher. Excavations during those three seasons uncovered six primary and two secondary burials, as well as an additional four intentional deposits of material culture not associated with any biological remains.[1]

The graves were dug into the soft sediment of the site and were blocked immediately after the burial with the same sediment removed in digging the grave; thus, it proved impossible to locate any evidence of the grave shafts or even identify the outlines of the burial chambers themselves, as the matrix immediately surrounding the burial was indistinguishable from the sediment elsewhere on the site. In each case, the nature of the burial chamber can only be ascertained by the layout of the body in relation to the blocking wall in those graves where the stones were present, as discussed further below.

None of the Gesher graves were disturbed in antiquity; only Graves 15 and 22, which were disturbed by modern activities at the site, did not preserve the original depositional arrangement. In most cases, each grave contained an undisturbed single skeleton in primary anatomical position with the grave goods still in their original positions.[2] This level of preservation is only rarely attested for Middle Bronze Age burials and allows for detailed examination of the burial customs during the Middle Bronze Age on the individual level.

3.1.2 The Graves

Information is provided concerning three elements of each grave: the stone construction (when present), the skeleton, and the associated grave goods. Four types of illustrations accompany the text when applicable: a plan of the remains, field photographs of the burial *in situ*, technical drawings of the finds, and photos of the finds.

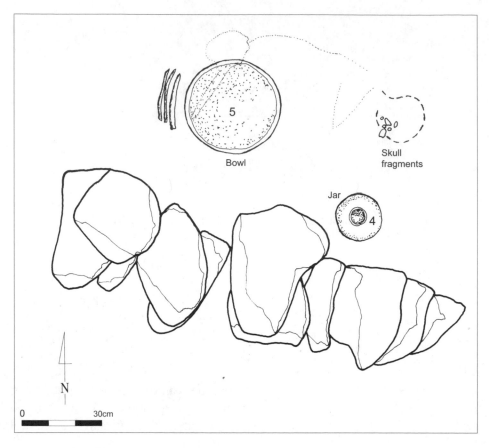

FIG. 3.1   *Plan of Grave 1.*

Grave 1

THE STONES: The stones with this grave were a carefully constructed row, three courses high, 160 cm long, 40 cm wide, and with a maximum height of 77 cm, with an east–west orientation (figs. 3.1–2). About 20 large basalt river pebbles were used in the construction. The stones were constructed south of the skeleton.

THE SKELETON: The burial was found in a very bad state of preservation. In the eastern part of the grave only a few teeth were found, indicating the original location of the head. In the western part, badly preserved long bones of the legs were found in a north–south direction, indicating that the skeleton had been in a flexed position. Based on better preserved skeletons in Graves 2, 5, 7, 8, 10–13, and 23, this information suggests here a primary burial, with the skeleton lying in an east–west orientation in a flexed position, with the head in the east facing south towards the stones, and the legs in the west.

THE GRAVE GOODS: Two grave goods were unearthed in association with the burial (figs. 3.3–4). A jar (Item 4) was found south of the skull and a large flat bowl (Item 5) was lying directly on the long bones. This is the only case at Gesher of a pottery vessel found lying directly on the bones.

Grave 2

THE STONES: A rectangular construction, carefully built, three to four courses high, 95 cm in length, 60 cm wide, and with a maximum height of 66 cm, on an east–west orientation, was found north of the skeleton (figs. 3.5–6). About 20 large and medium basalt river pebbles were used in the construction. The top of the stones was ca. 3.5 m below the current site surface.

Fig. 3.2   *The stone construction of Grave 1.*

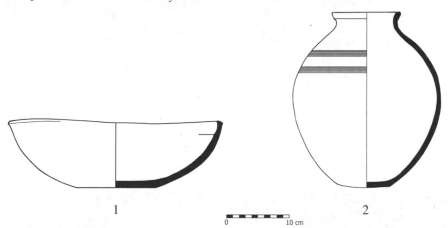

1   0   10 cm   2

Fig. 3.3   *Drawing of the assemblage from Grave 1.*

Fig. 3.4   *Photo of the assemblage from Grave 1.*

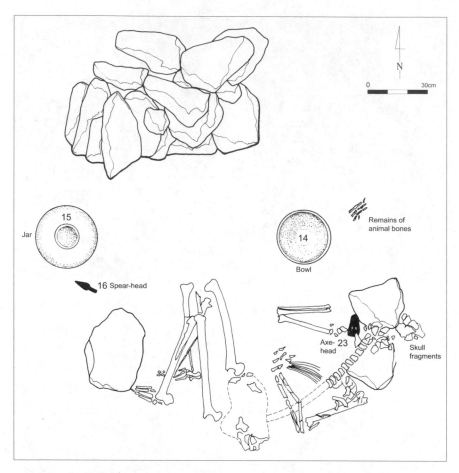

Fig. 3.5   *Plan of Grave 2.*

Fig. 3.6   *The stone construction of Grave 2.*

THE SKELETON: An individual primary burial, lying with the head in the east and the legs in the west was found in this grave (fig. 3.7). The left arm was flexed near the pelvis and the right arm was flexed near the head. The legs were in a flexed position with the knees facing north. Below the head two flat basalt stones were found, as if used as a pillow (fig. 3.8). The skull was badly preserved, and its fragments were found scatted around the grave. Near one foot a large flat basalt stone was found bordering the skeleton from the west. The corpse was lying on its right side, facing north toward the stones.

THE GRAVE GOODS: Two ceramic vessels and two bronze weapons were unearthed (figs. 3.9–10). Near the head a duckbill bronze axe (Item 23), a bowl (Item 14), and remains of animal bones were found. Near the legs a large jar (Item 15) and a bronze spearhcad (Item 16) were discovered. Some badly preserved wood fragments were still extant inside the axe. These fragments were sent for radiometric dating at the Oxford accelerating unit. The results from this test yielded a date of 3640+70 bp, uncalibrated (see fig 1.3).

FIG. 3.7   *The skeleton of Grave 2.*

FIG. 3.8   *Close-up of the fragmentary skull and the duckbill axe.*

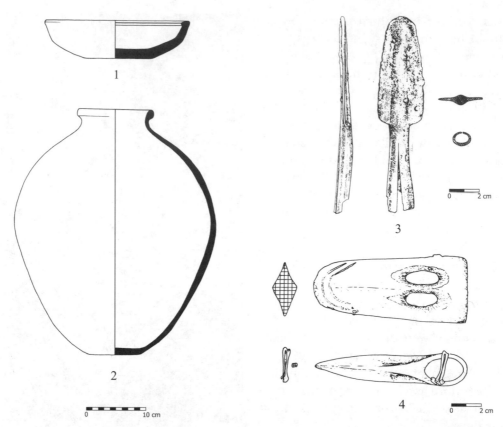

FIG. 3.9 *Drawing of the assemblage from Grave 2.*

FIG. 3.10 *Photo of the assemblage from Grave 2.*

Grave 3

The Stones: Two large basalt stones were found, one on top of the other (figs. 3.11–12). The stones were constructed east of the skeleton.

The Skeleton: Remains of one skeleton in secondary deposition were present in the grave. The bones were in a pile with the skull placed on top of the pelvis and various other bones, none of which were in anatomical order.

The Grave Goods: One small bowl (Item 10) was uncovered, upside down, south of the bones (figs. 3.13–14).

Grave 4A

In Grave 4, three activity levels were identified, two of them associated with human remains (fig. 3.15). In the upper level a concentration of stones was found together with three bowls (figs. 3.16–17). No skeletal remains were found at this level. In the central level, some 60 cm lower, one burial was found together with a perforated bone. In the lowest level, some further 50 cm lower, one burial was found with three pottery vessels nearby. Our suggestion is to view the upper and central levels as one grave, Grave 4A, with the lowest level designated as Grave 4B.

The Stones: Seven large and medium size basalt stones were loosely constructed in one row, with two courses, in a northeast to southwest direction. Their dimensions were 100 cm long, 30 cm wide, with a maximum height of 44 cm. The top of the stones was about 1 m below the current site surface. The stones were constructed above the skeleton.

The Skeleton: Either a secondary or partly disturbed primary single burial was found in this grave (fig. 3.18).

The Grave Goods: Adjacent to the skeleton a perforated bone was found (Item 21). It was discovered during sieving of the grave sediment, so its exact location in relation to the skeleton is not known. In addition, the three bowls (Items 1, 2, 3) unearthed on the upper level are related to this burial as well (figs. 3.19–20).

Grave 4B

The Stones: No stones can be related to this burial.

The Skeleton: The skeleton in this grave was found about 50 cm below the skeleton in Grave 4A (figs. 3.21–22). This was a primary single burial with the skeleton lying in a flexed position on its right side, with the head in the east and the legs in the west, face and knees to the north. The right arm was flexed near the head and the left arm near the chest.

The Grave Goods: Three vessels were unearthed; two jars were found near the head, to the south (Items 17, 18), and a bowl was located near the knees, to the north (Item 19; figs. 3.23–24). Some animal bones were found near the head, to the north.

Grave 5

The Stones: The upper part of the stone construction associated with this grave was eroded, and stones were found scattered and "floating" without a clear pattern. After removing this layer, the lower part of the construction was found in a good state of preservation (figs. 3.25–26). The wall was carefully constructed from about 20 large and medium-sized square basalt river pebbles, 85 cm long, 80 cm wide, and with a maximum height of about 1 m. The southern edge had two to three courses, while the northern was deeper and had five to six courses. This indicates that the base of the shaft was not flat but sloped toward the north. The top of the stones was about 2 m below the current site surface. The stones were constructed south of the skeleton.

The Skeleton: A primary single burial was found with its legs in a flexed position (fig. 3.27). The skeleton was lying in an east–west direction, with the head in the east and the legs in the west, on its left side, face and knees to the south. The arms were not flexed but in an extended position, parallel to the body. Two medium size flat basalt stones were found on the skull.

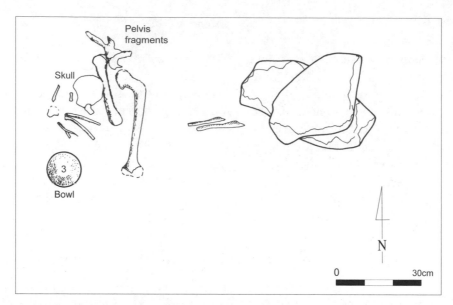

FIG. 3.11 *Plan of Grave 3.*

FIG. 3.12 *The stones of Grave 3.*

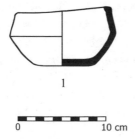

FIG. 3.13 *Drawing of the assemblage from Grave 3.*

FIG. 3.14 *Photo of the assemblage from Grave 3.*

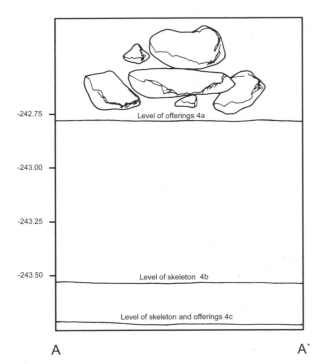

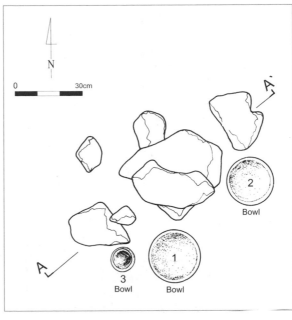

FIG. 3.15 *Section of Grave 4.*

FIG. 3.16 *Plan of Grave 4A, the upper phase.*

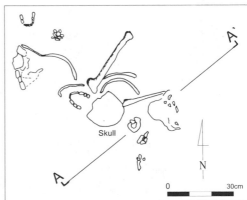

FIG. 3.17 *The stone construction and assemblage from Grave 4A, upper phase.*

FIG. 3.18 *Plan of Grave 4A, the lower phase.*

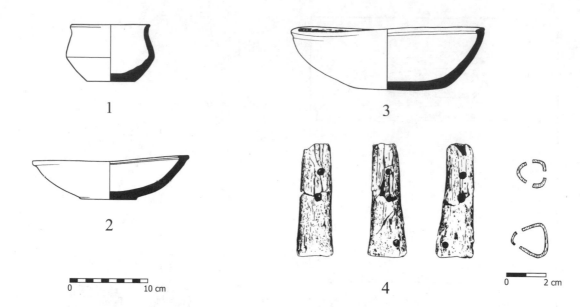

FIG. 3.19 *Drawing of the assemblage from Grave 4A.*

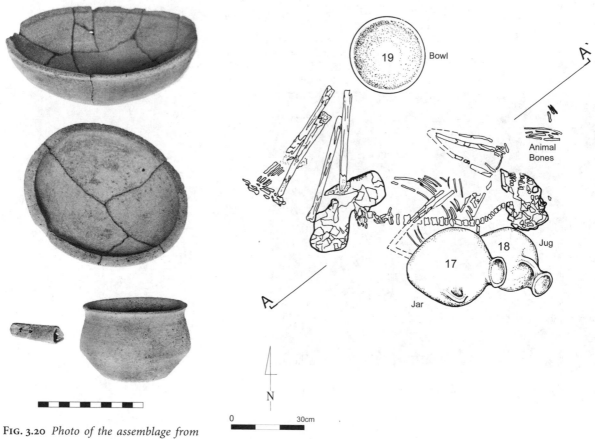

FIG. 3.20 *Photo of the assemblage from Grave 4A.*

FIG. 3.21 *Plan of Grave 4B.*

FIG. 3.22 *The skeleton of Grave 4A and, below, the assemblage from Grave 4B.*

THE GRAVE GOODS: Two offerings were found; a jar (Item 13) near the feet in the west and a bronze toggle pin (Item 12; figs. 3.28–29). The toggle pin was lying on the breast of the individual in the same orientation as the body, with its "mushroom-" shaped head in the west and the pointed edge in the east, towards the head.

Grave 6

This designation was given to a concentration of five medium-size basalt stones, loosely scattered without any clear construction or orientation. The top of the stones was about 50 cm below the current site surface. Further excavation around and below the stones in a diameter of 2 m did not uncover any skeletal remains or grave goods. It seems that the stones may be the last remains of a completely eroded grave (figs. 3.30–31).

Grave 7

THE STONES: No stone construction was found associated with Grave 7. This may be related to its location near the cliff – the stones may have been exposed to the surface and eroded away down the slope.

THE SKELETON: A primary single burial in flexed position was found (fig. 3.32). It was lying in an east–west orientation, with the head in the east, the legs in the west, and the face to the south. The skull was found lying on a medium-size flat basalt stone as if it was used as a pillow (fig. 3.33). Both arms were in a flexed position near the head. The legs, which were excavated later, were in a flexed position with the knees in the south (fig. 3.34). The burial was found 2.5 m below the current site surface.

THE GRAVE GOODS: Three offerings were found near the skeleton: a juglet (Item 11) near the head, a jar (Item 20) near the knees, and inside the jar a perforated bone (Item 22; fig. 3.35).

Grave 8

THE STONES: No stones were located in association with this grave.

THE SKELETON: A primary single burial in a flexed position was found (fig. 3.36). It was lying in an east–west orientation, with the head in the east and

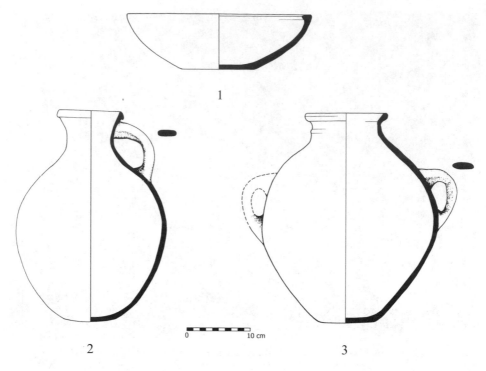

FIG. 3.23 *Drawing of the assemblage from Grave 4B.*

FIG. 3.24 *Photo of the assemblage from Grave 4B.*

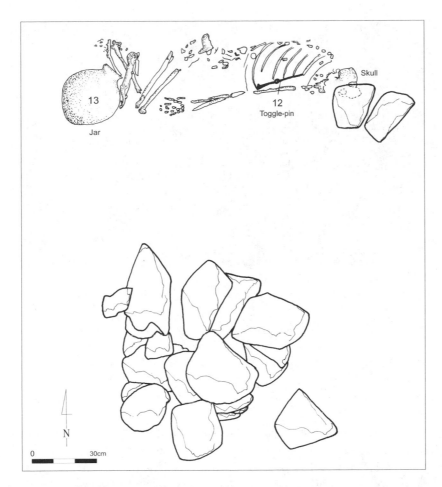

FIG. 3.25 *Plan of Grave 5.*

FIG. 3.26 *The stone construction of Grave 5.*

Fig. 3.27 *The skeleton and assemblage of Grave 5.*

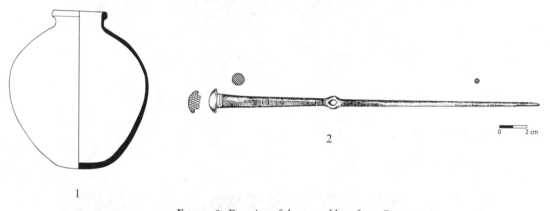

1

2

Fig. 3.28 *Drawing of the assemblage from Grave 5.*

Fig. 3.29 *Photo of the assemblage from Grave 5.*

the legs in the west, on its left side, face and knees to the south. The arms were in a flexed position near the head. The burial was found about 1 m below the current site surface.

THE GRAVE GOODS: Three ceramic vessels were found, two jars (Items 6 and 7) and a bowl (Item 8), all arranged around the skull on the south and east (figs. 3.37–38).

Grave 9

THE STONES: One stone was found at the site surface, together with a few exposed pottery sherds (fig. 3.39). The stone was located south of the skeleton.

THE SKELETON: This burial was found in an extremely fragmentary state of preservation; instead of bones, only a whitish powder was found. Small remnants of the skull were found in the east, with the teeth in the south. Near the skull some of the bones of the arms were observed. Based on the better preserved skeletons (Graves 2, 5, 7, 8, 10, 11, 12, and 13) it seems that this was a primary burial in an east–west alignment with the head in the east and the legs in flexed position in the west.

THE GRAVE GOODS: Four pottery vessels were found: one bowl near the stone (Item 24), two small bowls (Items 31 and 32) near the head on the south, and a small jar (Item 33; figs. 3.40–41).

Grave 10

THE STONES: No stone construction was associated with this grave. Near the heads of the burials, however, two large basalt stones were found; the northern stone was standing on its narrow side and the southern stone was lying flat.

THE SKELETONS: Two burials were found, making this the only grave with more than one skeleton (fig. 3.42). The southern skeleton (10B) was found in a primary position, following an east–west orientation with the head to the east and the legs in the west. The skeleton was lying on its left side, with flexed legs and the knees to the south. The arms were in a flexed position near the head.

The second skeleton (10A) was found adjacent to and north of the first, partly in primary and partly

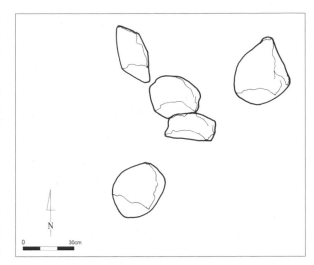

FIG. 3.30 *Plan of Grave 6.*

FIG. 3.31 *The stones of Grave 6.*

in secondary position. The lower half of the body was in the correct anatomical position, the legs flexed with the knees to the south. The bones of the upper half of the skeleton had been collected and redeposited; the skull was found lying on the pelvis and the arm bones were found around the pelvis to the north.

It seems clear that the burials in this grave were deposited in two stages. First, skeleton 10A was

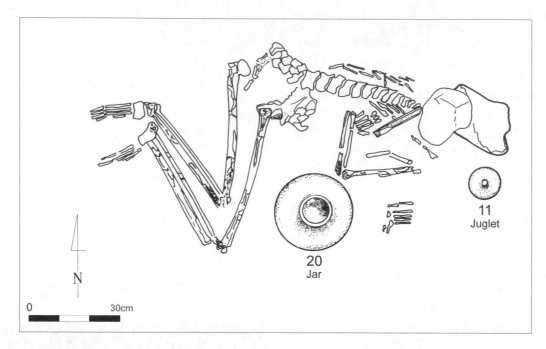

FIG. 3.32 *Plan of Grave 7.*

FIG. 3.33 *The skull resting on a stone in Grave 7.*

FIG. 3.34 *The lower part of the skeleton in Grave 7.*

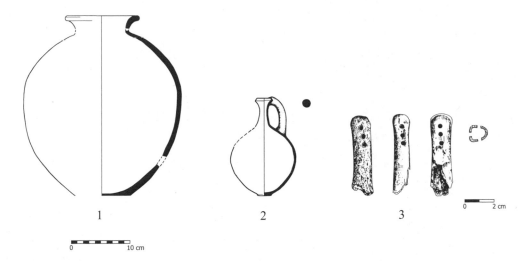

1   2   3

0   10 cm

Fig. 3.35 *Drawing of the assemblage from Grave 7.*

buried, with the head to the east and the legs in a flexed position to the west. Some time later, but after the flesh from skeleton 10A had completely decomposed, the grave was reopened and reused. In order to clear an area in which to place 10B, parts of 10A were removed and rearranged. This situation cannot be considered a secondary burial, since the rearrangement of the skeleton was not part of the official burial ritual but an outcome of the reuse of the limited burial space inside the grave.

The Grave Goods: The offerings of both burials, mainly pottery vessels, were organized in the south of the grave in a semi-circle (figs. 3.43–44). They include, from east to west, a jar (Item 25), a bowl with animal bones (Item 26), a small carinated bowl (Item 27) that was found inside the previous bowl, a jar (Item 28), a large bowl (Item 29), a jug (Item 30), and another carinated bowl (Item 35). This last bowl was found in a fragmentary state of preservation and it seems that it belongs to the first burial and was broken when the second burial was interred.

Grave 11

The Stones: The stones associated with this grave were found in a carefully constructed row of approximately 20 large and medium-size basalt river pebbles in an east–west direction, four to five courses high, 120 cm long, ca. 50 cm wide, and with

a maximum height of 52 cm (fig. 3.45). The stones were constructed south of the skeleton and found adjacent to it. The eastern edge of the stone row can be seen in the section of Area B (fig. 3.46).

The Skeleton: This was a primary burial in an east–west direction, with the head to the east and the legs in the west. The skeleton was lying on its left side, with flexed legs and the face and knees to the south, turned toward the stones. The arms were in a flexed position near the head. The skull was found about 15 cm east of its correct anatomical position.

The Grave Goods: One jar (Item 34) was found near the knees, adjacent to the stones (figs. 3.47–48).

Grave 12

The Stones: The stones in this grave consisted of a carefully constructed row of approximately 30 large and medium-size basalt river pebbles in an east–west direction, five to six courses high, 155 cm long, 60 cm wide, and with a maximum height of 84 cm (figs. 3.49–51). The top of the stones was immediately below the current site surface. The stones were constructed north of the skeleton.

The Skeleton: As in Graves 1 and 9, which were also found very close to the current surface, most of the bones of this skeleton were not preserved.

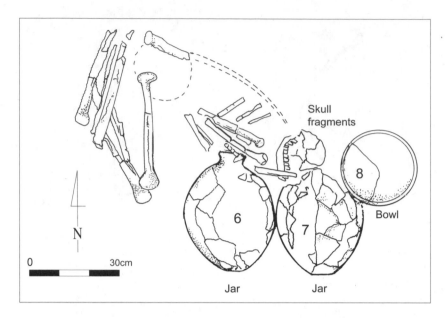

Fig. 3.36 *Plan of Grave 8.*

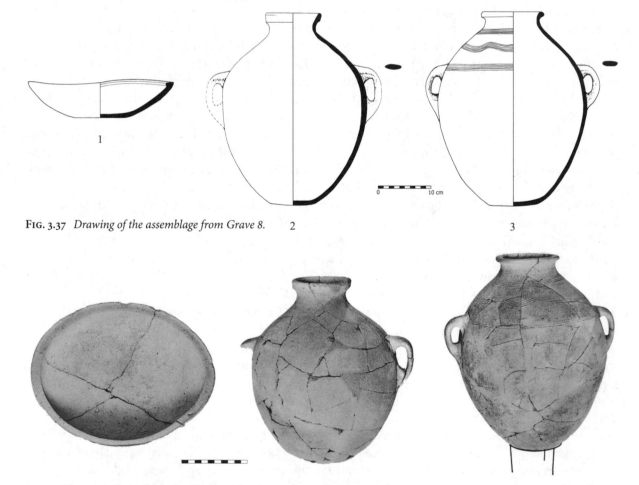

Fig. 3.37 *Drawing of the assemblage from Grave 8.*

Fig. 3.38 *Photo of the assemblage from Grave 8.*

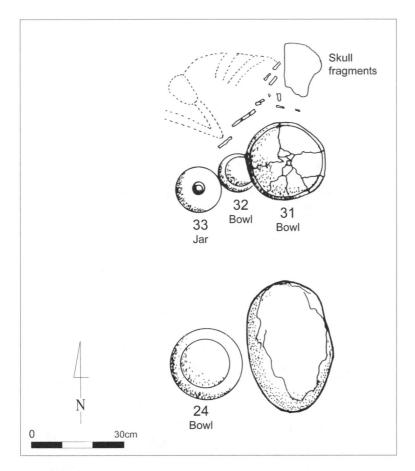

FIG. 3.39 *Plan of Grave 9.*

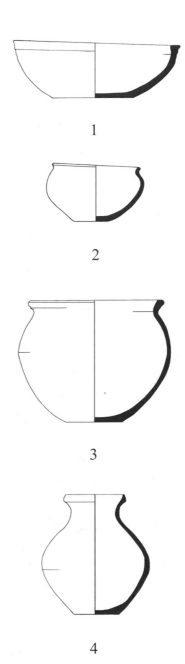

FIG. 3.40 *Drawing of the assemblage from Grave 9.*

FIG. 3.41 *Photo of the assemblage from Grave 9.*

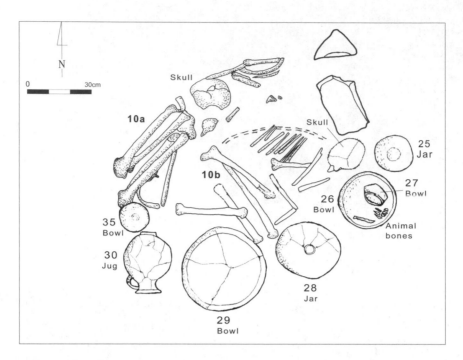

FIG. 3.42 *Plan of Grave 10.*

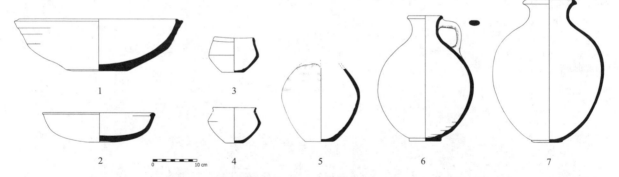

FIG. 3.43 *Drawing of the assemblage from Grave 10.*

FIG. 3.44 *Photo of the assemblage from Grave 10.*

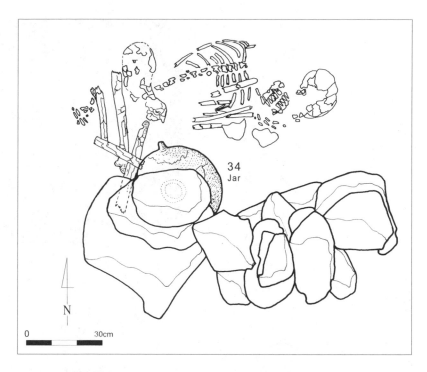

Fig. 3.45 *Plan of Grave 11.*

The few extant remains, however, indicate a primary single burial in an east–west orientation with the head in the east and the legs in the west. The skeleton lay on its right side with flexed legs, face and knees to the north. Parts of the arms were preserved and indicated that they were in a flexed position near the head.

The Grave Goods: Near the head and adjacent to the stones a jar (Item 36) and a bronze duckbill axe (Item 46) were unearthed (figs. 3.52–53). A bronze nail (Item 47) was found approximately 10 cm from the axe.

Grave 13

The Stones: No stones were found in association with this grave.

The Skeleton: A primary single burial in an east–west orientation with the head in the east and the legs in the west was found in the grave (figs. 3.54–55). The skull was lying on a medium-size flat basalt stone with the face to the north. The legs were in a flexed position with the knees to the north. The arms were in a flexed position near the head.

Fig. 3.46 *The stone construction and skeleton of Grave 11.*

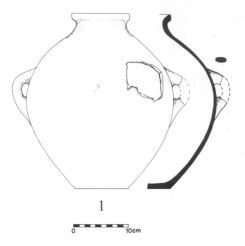

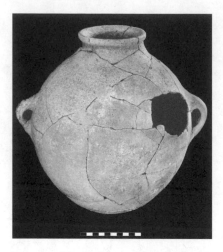

FIG. 3.47 *Drawing of the assemblage from Grave 11.*   **FIG. 3.48** *Photo of the assemblage from Grave 11.*

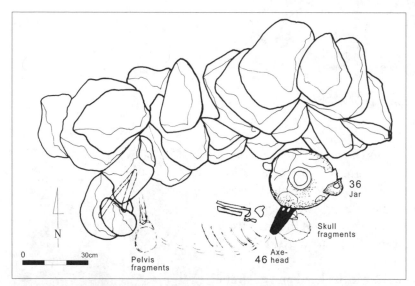

FIG. 3.49 *Plan of Grave 12.*

FIG. 3.50 *The stone construction of Grave 12 from the south.*

Fig. 3.51 *The stone construction of Grave 12 from above.*

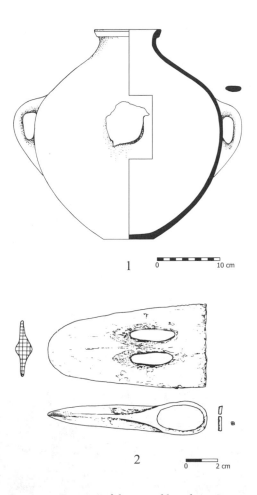

Fig. 3.52 *Drawing of the assemblage from Grave 12.*

Fig. 3.53 *Photo of the assemblage from Grave 12.*

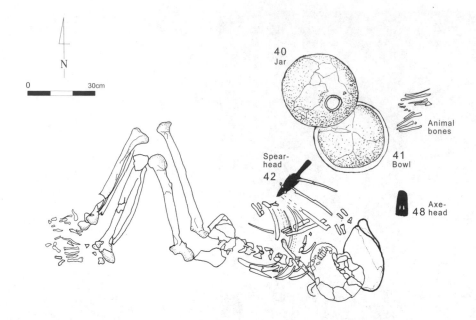

FIG. 3.54 *Plan of Grave 13.*

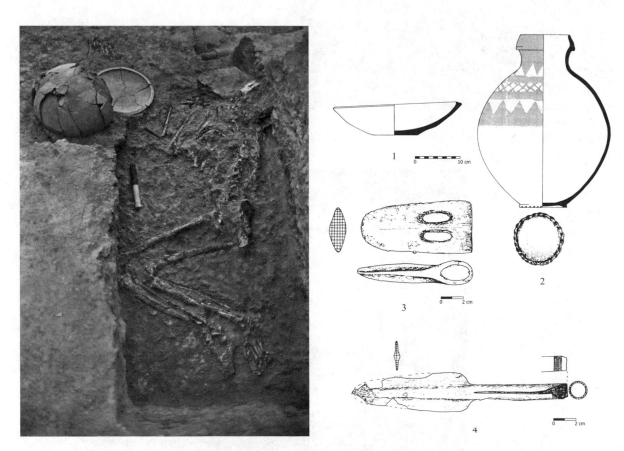

FIG. 3.55 *The skeleton and assemblage from Grave 13.*   **FIG. 3.56** *Drawing of the assemblage from Grave 13.*

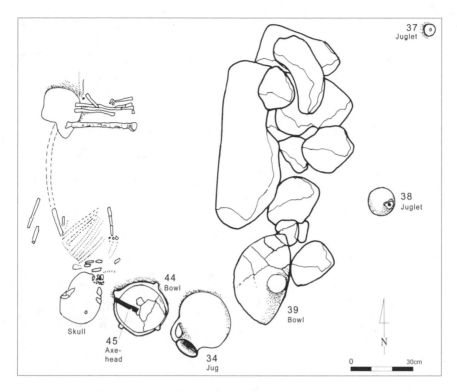

Fig. 3.57 *Plan of Grave 14.*

The Grave Goods: A bronze duckbill axe (Item 48) was located near the head to the east, and a bronze spearhead (Item 42) was found under the arms (fig. 3.56). Inside the spearhead some wood remains were still preserved; unfortunately, these were too fragmentary for any further analysis to be carried out. Near the chest, to the north, a painted jar (Item 40) and a bowl (Item 41) were found. Near the bowl, but outside of it, some animal remains were unearthed (see discussion in Chapter 10).

Grave 14

The Stones: The stones associated with this grave comprised a rectangular structure composed of two parallel stone rows, two to three courses high, 120 cm long, 60 cm wide, and with a maximum height of 68 cm (figs. 3.57–58). The top of the stones was about 50 m below the current site surface. The stones were constructed east of the skeleton.

The Skeleton: This grave contained a primary single burial, not very well preserved, with the head in the south and the legs in the north. The

Fig. 3.58 *The stone construction and upper layer of assemblage from Grave 14.*

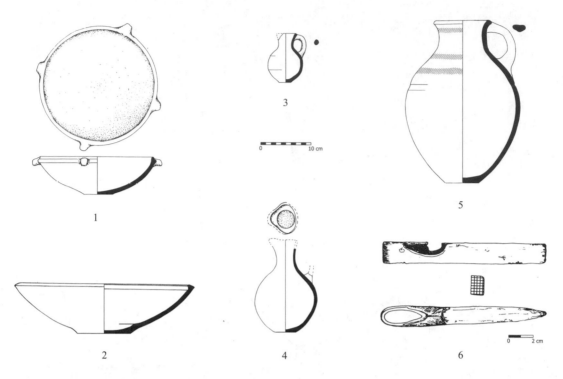

FIG. 3.59 *Drawing of the assemblage from Grave 14.*

FIG. 3.60 *Photo of the assemblage from Grave 14.*

skeleton lay with flexed legs with the knees to the east, toward the stones, and with the arms in a flexed position near the head.

The Grave Goods: Offerings were found on two levels; the lower level of offerings was near the skeleton and the upper one was on top of the stone construction (figs. 3.59–60). Adjacent to the skull in the south a jar (Item 43) and a bowl with four knobs on the rim (Item 44) were found; a bronze axe (Item 45) was found inside the bowl. On the stone construction three pottery vessels were unearthed: a small juglet (Item 37), a large juglet (Item 38), and a bowl (Item 39). The bowl was found upside down on the stones, with the juglets a few centimeters to the east.

Grave 15

This grave was destroyed by a local farmer. During a visit to the site some time after that damage, a concentration of pottery was found in one location, indicating the existence of another grave.

The Stones: Unknown

The Skeleton: Unknown.

The Grave Goods: Fragments of seven pottery vessels were collected (fig. 3.61). No information could be retrieved concerning their original location.

Grave 16

The Stones: No stones were found in association with this burial.

The Skeleton: Grave 16 was a secondary burial of an adult male, found relatively close to the surface (figs. 3.62–63). The bones were deposited in a tight group with the cranium placed on top of the pile.

The Grave Goods: Three vessels were found in association with the burial (figs. 3.64–65): a plainware jug with a trefoil mouth (Item 56), a handleless store jar (Item 58), and an incomplete small carinated

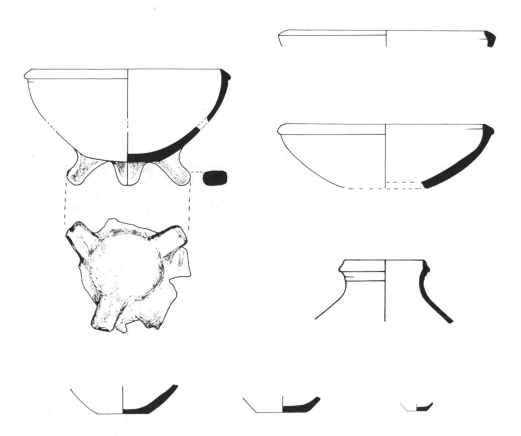

Fig. 3.61 *Drawing of the assemblage from Grave 15.*

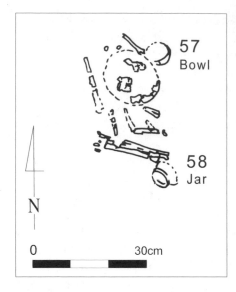

FIG. 3.62 *Drawing of Grave 16.*

FIG. 3.63 *Photo of Grave 16.*

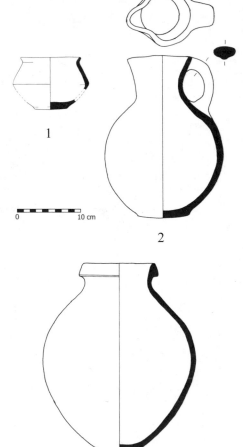

FIG. 3.64 *Drawing of the assemblage from Grave 16.*   FIG. 3.65 *Photo of the assemblage from Grave 16.*

FIG. 3.66 *View of stones and skeleton of Grave 17.*

bowl (Item 57). The jug was found at least 10 cm above the burial itself, and while most probably associated with the interment, it may have been placed there later than the secondary deposition of the burial itself. The partial remains of the bowl were located midway down in the pile of bones on the east side, and the jar was found with the rim just at the lowest level of the pile, also on the east side.

Grave 17

THE STONES: Three field stones were found in association with this burial. They were located to the northeast of the lower portion of the skeleton (fig. 3.66).

THE SKELETON: Grave 17 was a primary burial, probably of an adult female (figs. 3.67–68). The individual was lying in a flexed position on the right side of the body, with the head to the east and the face and knees to the north. The arms and hands were extremely poorly preserved, but the extant remains indicate that they were flexed in front of the chest.

THE GRAVE GOODS: Several ceramic vessels were excavated in association with the burial (figs. 3.69–70). Two incompletely preserved jars (Items 59 and 60) were excavated from near the feet of the individual.[3] In addition, an intact carinated bowl (Item 61) was excavated from in front of the arms, and a large open bowl (Item 63) was found in several large pieces and at different levels, also from the area around the individual's arms and chest. Two painted sherds (Item 64), most probably from a jug or jar, were also recovered in association with this burial. A small painted jar (Item 62) was excavated from the wash/erosion approximately half a meter to the east of the stones associated with the burial; it is not possible to tell if this piece should be considered as part of the burial assemblage interred with the individual.

Grave 18

THE STONES: A thick, L-shaped, stone construction was found in association with Grave 18. This feature, built of two to three courses of medium-sized field stones, was located to the north of the skeleton at the individual's feet and lower legs.

THE SKELETON: Grave 18 was a primary interment of an adult male, lying flexed on the right side, with the head to the south (figs. 3.71–72). This burial was extremely poorly preserved, and no information could be gained about the placement of the legs or arms. Given that the individual was lying on the

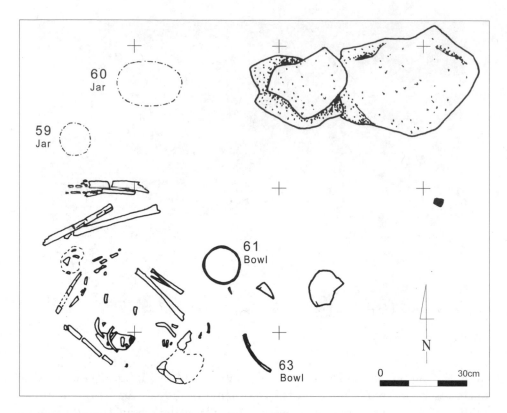

FIG. 3.67 *Drawing of Grave 17.*

FIG. 3.68 *Photo of Grave 17.*

right side, it may be suggested that the face and knees were towards the stones on the east near the legs of the burial.

The Grave Goods: A store jar (Item 67) and a painted jug (Item 68) were found near the individual's feet, and one spearhead (Item 66) was found to the southeast of the head; a third vessel, an open bowl (Item 65), was found placed upside-down at the lowest level of the stones of the installation on its north side and, thus, outside the blocked burial chamber (figs. 3.73–74).

Grave 19

The Stones: No trace of a blocked chamber was found in association with this burial, but one large basaltic stone was uncovered to the east of the lower body.

The Skeleton: Grave 19 was a primary interment of an adult male, flexed on the right side, with the head to the south and the face and knees to the east (figs. 3.75–76). The arms were flexed over the chest. In particular, the cranium and mandibles were found in a state of extremely good preservation (fig. 3.77).

The Grave Goods: Four ceramic vessels and one bronze spearhead were found with the burial (figs. 3.78–79). An almost completely intact two-handled store jar (Item 19) was located near the lower legs and feet; the spearhead (Item 71) was found angling upwards at the base of the jar (fig. 3.80). A carinated bowl (Item 70) was found some distance to the east

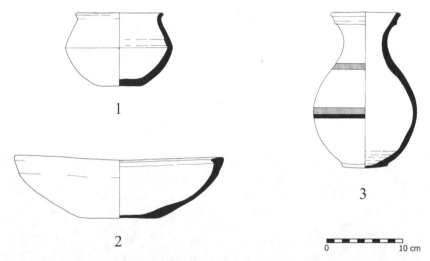

1

2

3

0   10 cm

FIG. 3.69 *Drawing of the assemblage from Grave 17.*

FIG. 3.70 *Photo of the assemblage from Grave 17.*

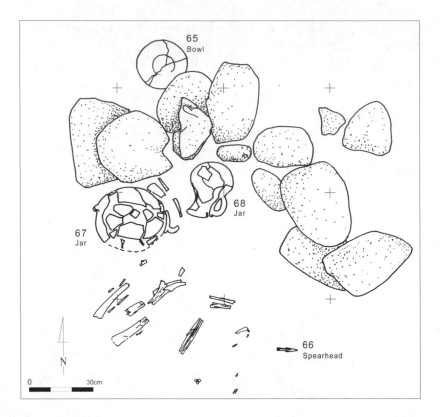

FIG. 3.71 *Drawing of Grave 18.*

FIG. 3.72 *Photo of Grave 18.*

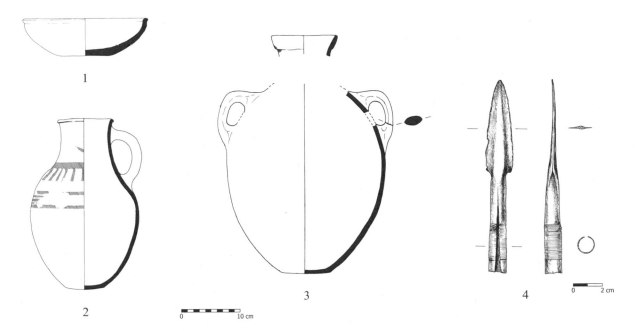

FIG. 3.73 *Drawing of the assemblage from Grave 18.*

of the legs. A hemispheric bowl (Item 72) and a large open bowl (Item 73) were excavated from the area in front of the individual's arms and chest.

Grave 20

THE STONES: No stones were found in association with the burial.

THE SKELETON: Grave 20 was a secondary deposition consisting of the bones gathered into a bundle or pile with the cranium placed on top (figs. 3.81–82).

THE GRAVE GOODS: Two ceramic vessels, a jar (Item 76) and a large open bowl (item 75; figs. 3.83–84), were uncovered in proximity a little to the east of the burial and may be presumed to be associated with it, although these vessels were some distance from the burial and the sherds were spread out over a larger area (fig. 3.85).

Grave 21

THE STONES: No stones were found in relation to this burial.

THE SKELETON: This was a primary interment of an adult female, flexed on the right side, with

FIG. 3.74 *Photo of the assemblage from Grave 18.*

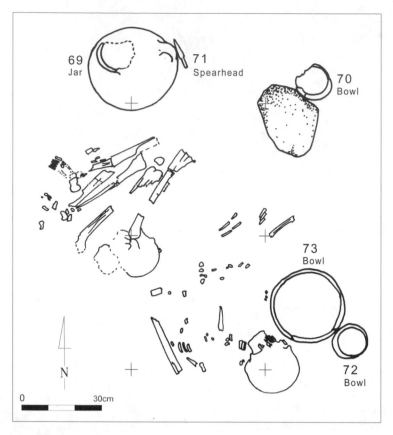

FIG. 3.75 *Drawing of Grave 19.*

FIG. 3.76 *Photo of Grave 19.*

FIG. 3.77 *Close-up of cranium from Grave 19.*

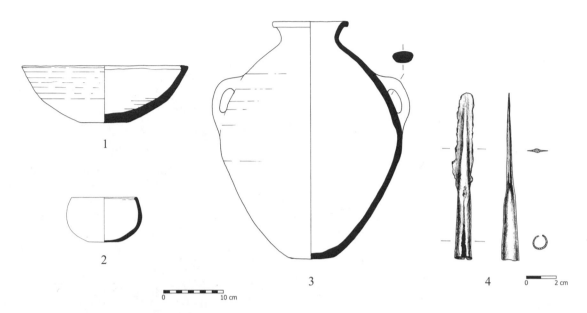

FIG. 3.78 *Drawing of the assemblage from Grave 19.*

FIG. 3.79 *Photo of the assemblage from Grave 19.*

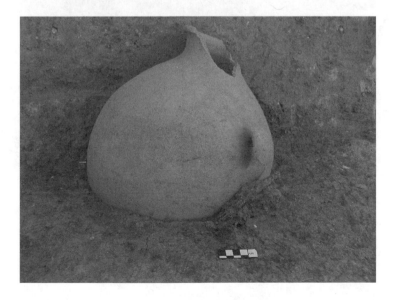

FIG. 3.80 *Photo of store-jar and spearhead from Grave 19 in situ.*

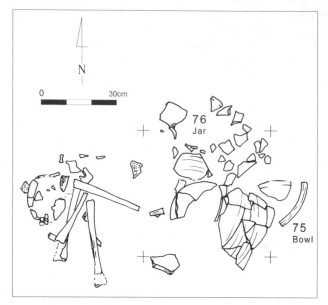

FIG. 3.81 *Drawing of Grave 20.*

FIG. 3.82 *Photo of Grave 20.*

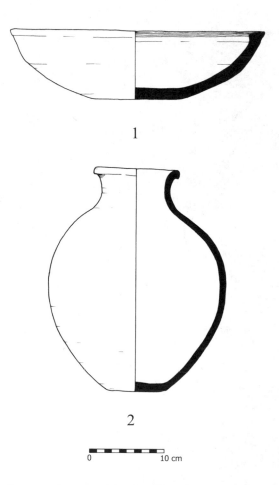

FIG. 3.83 *Drawing of the assemblage from Grave 20.*

FIG. 3.84 *Photo of the assemblage from Grave 20.*

FIG. 3.85 *View of Grave 20 and ceramics* in situ.

the head to the east and the face and knees to the north (fig. 3.86). The skeleton was extremely poorly preserved; no traces of the hands or feet could be found.

THE GRAVE GOODS: A broken but complete store jar (Item 78) was placed near the feet of the individual, and a large open bowl (Item 79) containing faunal remains was found in front of the arms and chest area (figs. 3.87–88; see also discussion in Chapter 10).

Grave 22

THE STONES: No stones were found in relation to the burial.

THE SKELETON: Grave 22 was extremely badly preserved and partially destroyed by both erosion and the road cut; as a result, it was possible to recover only a small portion of the skeleton. What bones were extant, however, indicated a primary burial, possibly of a male individual lying in a flexed position on the left side, with the head to the south (fig. 3.89).

THE GRAVE GOODS: No ceramic vessels were found in association with the body. A bronze spearhead (Item 77) was found lying under the right lower arm (fig. 3.90).

Grave 23

THE STONES: A stone wall approximately four courses high, two courses wide, and a meter in length was found to the south of the skeleton. This wall leaned slightly from south to north, with the burial chamber itself located on the north side.

THE SKELETON: Grave 23 was an extremely well-preserved primary interment of an adult male lying flexed on the left side, with the head to the east and the face and knees to the south (figs. 3.91–92). The arms were flexed over the body.

THE GRAVE GOODS: A medium-sized handleless store jar (Item 81) and an open bowl (Item 82)

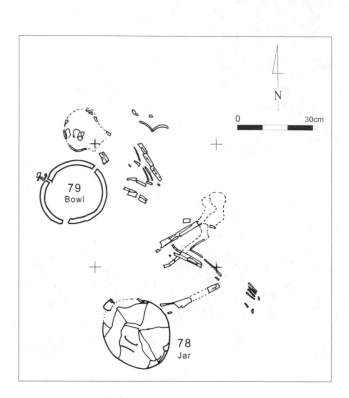

Fig. 3.86 *Drawing of Grave 21.*

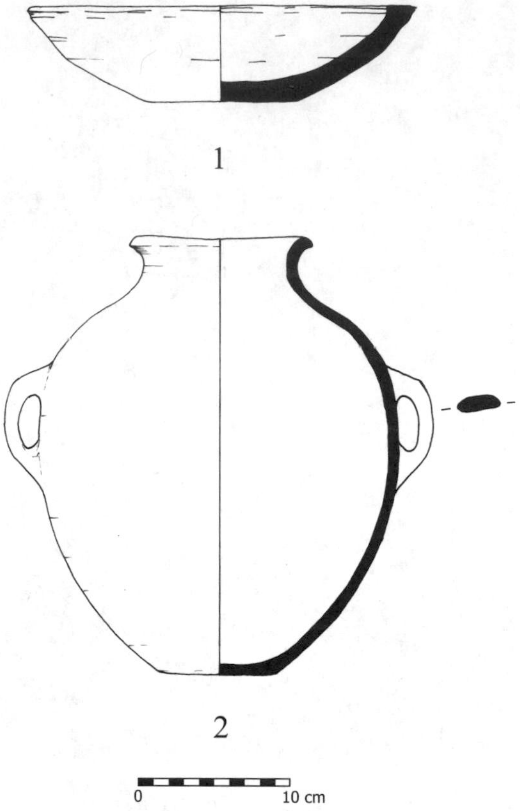

Fig. 3.87 *Drawing of the assemblage from Grave 21.*

Fig. 3.88 *Photo of the assemblage from Grave 21.*

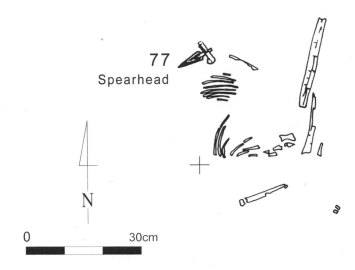

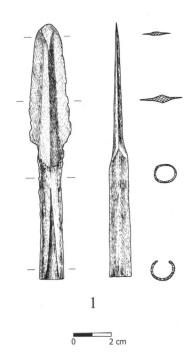

Fig. 3.89 *Drawing of Grave 22.*

Fig. 3.90 *Drawing of the assemblage from Grave 22.*

were found in association with Grave 23 (figs. 3.93–94). The jar was placed near the lower legs and feet of the individual, and the bowl, which contained a large quantity of faunal remains, was found near the arms in front of the burial (see Chapter 10).

3.1.3 *The Depositions without Skeletal Remains*

Deposition 1

Deposition 1 consisted of a group of three stones and two ceramic vessels. Two of the stones were placed adjacent to one another, with the third a short distance to the east. The ceramics, a small bottle (Item 53) placed inside a thick hemispheric bowl (Item 54), were found at the southeastern extent of the stone grouping (fig. 3.95).

Deposition 2

This deposition consisted of one medium-sized rock with a small carinated bowl (Item 52) placed nearby (fig. 3.96).

Deposition 3

This deposition consisted solely of part of a small broken bowl (Item 55) lying in otherwise empty fill.

No stones were found in association with this vessel, which was incomplete and so badly preserved as to not be restorable.

Deposition 4

Deposition 4 consisted of a small red-slipped jar (Item 85) lying inside a large open bowl (Item 86) (fig. 3.97).[4] A small, incomplete carinated bowl (Item 84) was found approximately 30 to 40 cm to the west of these two vessels in the disturbed and heavily eroded area of the upper slope and may be associated with this grouping, but this cannot be determined with any certainty (fig. 3.98). No stones were found with this deposition.

3.2. Summary of the Burials

The interments from the excavations at Gesher may be divided into three categories: 1) primary burials, 2) secondary depositions, and 3) intentional deposits of material culture found separately from any identifiable skeletal remains.

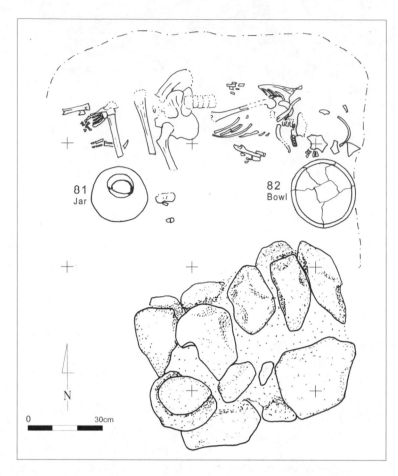

FIG. 3.91 *Drawing of Grave 23.*

FIG. 3.92 *Photo of Grave 23.*

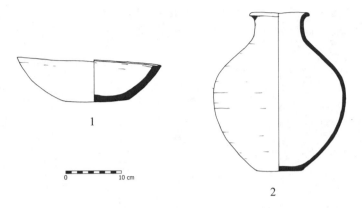

FIG. 3.93 *Drawing of the assemblage from Grave 23.*

FIG. 3.94 *Photo of the assemblage from Grave 23.*

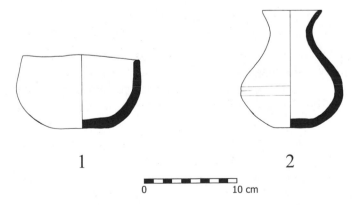

FIG. 3.95 *Drawing of the assemblage from Deposition 1.*

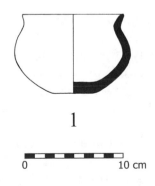

FIG. 3.96 *Drawing of the assemblage from Deposition 2.*

FIG. 3.97 *Photo of Deposition 4.*

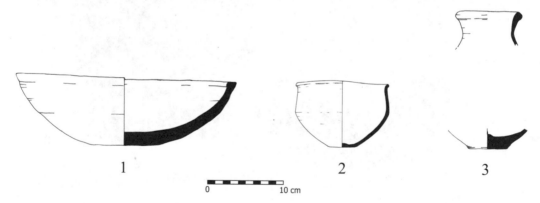

FIG. 3.98 *Drawing of the assemblage from Deposition 4.*

3.2.1 *The Primary Burials*

The majority of the burials excavated at Gesher were primary depositions, all of adult individuals; no child or infant burials were discovered at the site. In every case, with the exception of Grave 10 which contained two skeletons, the primary burial contained a single individual lying in a flexed position. There is not, however, any specific discernable pattern regarding orientation, the side on which the individual was lying, or the number and placement of grave goods around the body.

Of the nineteen primary burials, sixteen were oriented with their head to the east, while four were placed with the head to the south. Burial in a flexed position with the head to the east also characterizes the Middle Bronze Age burials at Dhahrat el-Humraiya (Ory 1948: 77). At Gesher, the four individuals oriented to the south were all male and fit the "warrior burial" type of grave common in the Levant; in the three other "warrior burials" from the cemetery, the bodies were buried with the head towards the east, and, thus, it is not possible to link a specific class of burial with a particular orientation.

Although all of the "warrior burials" were lying on their right side, other individuals were placed on their right side as well. The side on which the individual was lying seems to have been linked to the construction of the burial chamber itself; in those burials where a blocking wall or group of stones was excavated, the individual was lying with the face towards the wall, or entrance, to the chamber (see also Garfinkel and Bonfil 1990).[5]

Although all of the burials were found with associated material remains, no specific consistent pattern could be discerned regarding the nature of the grave goods or their placement around the body. The items in each burial ranged from one to five objects, and at least one ceramic vessel was found with each burial, with the exception of Grave 22. The grave goods included metals, worked bone, and faunal remains. In general, larger vessels, such as jars and jugs, were placed near the feet of the individual, and smaller items, both ceramic and metal, were placed around the region of the chest and head, although there was no consistent pattern in the placement of objects in the grave (Table 3.1).

3.2.2   The Secondary Burials

Three of the burials excavated at Gesher, Graves 3, 16, and 20, were clearly secondary deposits.[6] In each deposit, the long bones and other large bones, such as the pelvis, sacrum, etc., had been collected and placed in a pile with the cranium deposited on top.[7] From the manner of collection and subsequent redeposition, as well as the material culture found in association, it is clear that these were intentional deposits. It is likely that these secondary burials resulted when the people using the cemetery encountered an older grave while digging a new one, collected the extant bones from the older skeleton, and reburied them together with the associated material culture.

It is important to note that, generally, secondary burial is an uncommon practice in the Middle Bronze Age (Hallote 1995: 103). The rarity of the practice, as compared to its relative frequency in the preceding EB IV/MB I, has led to suggestions that secondary burials more typically represent

semi-nomadic pastoralist societies, as opposed to the primary depositions associated with more sedentary populations (Hallote 1995; Ilan 1995; Dever 1987). The presence of three unambiguous secondary burials at Gesher, with associated material culture of clear MB IIA character, therefore, contradicts this presumed clear-cut division of burial types from the EB IV/MB I to MB IIA, and also raises certain interpretive issues regarding the nature of the Gesher cemetery and the early MB IIA in this region (see discussion in Chapter 11).

3.2.3   The Depositions without Skeletal Remains

The depositions without skeletal remains excavated from the site are all intentional deposits of material culture not associated with any biological remains.[8] In each case, there was no evidence of other human activity in the area, and no pit or shaft lines were found around any of these deposits. While it is possible that these finds may be the result of post-depositional movement on the hillside, perhaps from erosion, none of the four deposits appeared tipped or to have slid in any way, and the matrix in which they were found also showed no evidence of erosion.

One possible explanation for the depositions is that the skeletal remains associated with this material were simply no longer extant by the time of excavation. Given the poor nature of skeletal preservation at the site, especially at higher elevations and close to the slope of the hill – a criterion that fits each of these four depositions – it is possible that the associated biological remains could have deteriorated completely prior to the excavations. It should also be noted that if the associated remains belonged to a young individual, these bones would be considerably more fragile and would deteriorate faster. To date, only adult individuals have been found at the Gesher cemetery, and it is possible that the depositions may represent the burials of younger individuals that have not been preserved, although this is purely speculative.

Another possible explanation for these four groups of ceramics is their location in relation to other burials found in the area. No proper evidence of a tomb shaft has ever satisfactorily been found

Table 3.1 Inventory of the grave goods from the burials.

Item	Grave	Description	Levels (upper / lower)	Figure
1	G-4A	Bowl	-242.71 / -242.77	Fig. 3.19:1
2	G-4A	Bowl	-242.69 / -242.78	Fig. 3.19:2
3	G-4A	Bowl	-242.70 / -242.77	Fig. 3.19:3
4	G-1	Jar	-241.64 / -241.80	Fig. 3.3:2
5	G-1	Bowl	-241.88 / -241.91	Fig. 3.3:1
6	G-8	Jar	-237.45 / -237.70	Fig. 3.7:2
7	G-8	Jar	-237.55 / -237.64	Fig. 3.7:3
8	G-8	Bowl	-237.61 / -237.66	Fig. 3.7:1
9	G-8	Sherds, restored with Items 6–8	-237.50 / -237.70	NA
10	G-3	Bowl	-241.18 / -241.10	Fig. 3.13:1
11	G-7	Juglet	-245.07 / -245.12	Fig. 3.35:2
12	G-5	Bronze toggle pin	-245.57 / -245.58	Fig. 3.28:2
13	G-5	Jar	-245.35 / -245.63	Fig. 3.28:1
14	G-2	Bowl	-244.75 / -244.84	Fig. 3.9:1
15	G-2	Jar	244.74 / -244.85	Fig. 3.9:2
16	G-2	Bronze spearhead	244.77 / -244.79	Fig. 3.9:3
17	G-4B	Jar	243.52 / -243.66	Fig. 3.23:3
18	G-4B	Jug	-243.37 / -243.73	Fig. 3.23:2
19	G-4B	Bowl	-243.73 / -243.79	Fig. 3.23:1
20	G-7	Jar	-244.92 / -245.14	Fig. 3.35:1
21	G-4A	Perforated bone	-243.44 / -243.64	Fig. 3.19:4
22	G-7	Perforated bone, in 20	-244.92 / -245.14	Fig. 3.35:3
23	G2	Bronze duckbill axe with nail	-244.78 / -244.80	Fig. 3.9:4
24	G-9	Bowl	-240.62 / -240.81	Fig. 3.40:3
25	G-10	Painted jar	Not measured	Fig. 3.43:5
26	G-10	Bowl	Not measured	Fig. 3.43:2
27	G-10	Bowl, inside # 26	Not measured	Fig. 3.43:4
28	G-10	Jar	-243.37 / -243.55	Fig. 3.43:7
29	G-10	Bowl	-243.47 / -243.58	Fig. 3.43:1
30	G-10	Jug	-243.40 / -243.51	Fig. 3.43:6
31	G-9	Bowl	-241.17 / -241.34	Fig. 3.40:1
32	G-9	Bowl	-241.18 / -241.26	Fig. 3.40:2
33	G-9	Small jar	-241.13 / -241.27	Fig. 3.40:4
34	G-11	Jar	-241.53 / -241.78	Fig. 3.47:1
35	G-10	Bowl	-243.52 / -243.57	Fig. 3.43:3
36	G-12	Jar	-241.95 / -242.22	Fig. 3.52:1
37	G-14	Juglet	-241.08 / -241.20	Fig. 3.59:3
38	G-14	Juglet	-240.86 / -241.02	Fig. 3.59:4
39	G-14	Bowl	-240.84 / -241.04	Fig. 3.59:2
40	G-13	Painted jar	-241.92 / -242.23	Fig. 3.56:2
41	G-13	Bowl	-242.25 / -242.27	Fig. 3.56:1
42	G-13	Bronze spearhead	-242.20 / -242.22	Fig. 3.56:4
43	G-14	Jug	-241.09 / -241.38	Fig. 3.59:5

Table 3.1 (continued). Inventory of the grave goods from the burials.

Item	Grave	Description	Levels (upper / lower)	Figure
44	G-14	Knob bowl	-241.29 / -241.38	Fig. 3.59:1
45	G-14	Bronze axe	-241.32 / -241.37	Fig. 3.59:6
46	G-12	Bronze duckbill axe	-242.18 / -242.22	Fig. 3.52:2
47	G-12	Bronze nail	-242.10 / -242.10	Fig. 3.52:2
48	G-13	Bronze duckbill axe	-242.23 / -242.26	Fig. 3.56:3
49	Topsoil	Bronze spearhead	—	NA
50	G-15	Pottery fragments	Topsoil	Fig. 3.61
51	Cleaning	Bowl	Not measured	NA
52	Deposition 2	Bowl	-242.32 / -242.39	Fig. 3.96:1
53	Deposition 1	Bottle	-241.70 / -241.81	Fig. 3.95:2
54	Deposition 1	Bowl	-241.70 / -241.81	Fig. 3.95:1
55	Deposition 3	Bowl fragments, not drawn	-241.80 / -241.88	NA
56	G-16	Jug	-241.13 / -241.28	Fig. 3.64:2
57	G-16	Carinated bowl	-242.21 / -241.28	Fig. 3.64:1
58	G-16	Jar	-241.31 / -241.60	Fig. 3.64:3
59	G-17	Jar, body only / not drawn	-242.27 / -242.40	NA
60	G-17	Jar, base only / not drawn	-241.27 / -241.33	NA
61	G-17	Carinated bowl	-241.38 / -241.44	Fig. 3.69:1
62	Wash / G-17	Painted jar	-242.27 / -242.46	Fig. 3.69:3
63	G-17	Bowl	-241.40 / -241.53	Fig. 3.69:2
64	G-17	Painted sherds	-241.17 / -241.36	NA
65	G-18	Bowl	-241.40 / -241.62	Fig. 3.73:1
66	G-18	Bronze spearhead	-241.59 / -241.62	Fig. 3.73:4
67	G-18	Jar	-241.40 / -241.62	Fig. 3.73:3
68	G-18	Painted jug	-241.58 / -241.67	Fig. 3.73:2
69	G-19	Jar	-241.78 / -242.18	Fig. 3.78:3
70	G-19	Carinated bowl	-241.94 / -242.00	NA
71	G-19	Bronze spearhead	-241.92 / -242.00	Fig. 3.78:4
72	G-19	Bowl	-242.02 / -242.15	Fig. 3.78:2
73	G-19	Bowl	-242.00 / -242.09	Fig. 3.78:1
74	Cleaning	Red-slipped jug	No measurements	NA
75	G-20	Bowl	-243.38 / -243.44	Fig. 3.83:1
76	G-20	Jar	-243.33 / -243.42	Fig. 3.83:2
77	G-22	Bronze Spearhead	-243.36 / -243.39	Fig. 3.90:1
78	G-21	Jar	-242.01 / -242.22	Fig. 3.87:2
79	G-21	Bowl	-242.12 / -242.24	Fig. 3.87:1
80	G-21	Faunal remains	-242.12 / -242.24	NA
81	G-23	Jar	-242.45 / -242.74	Fig. 3.93:2
82	G-23	Bowl	-242.56 / -242.68	Fig. 3.93:1
83	G-23	Faunal remains	-242.56 / -242.67	NA
84	Deposition 4	Bowl	-241.53 / -241.67	Fig. 3.98:2
85	Deposition 4	Red slipped jar	-241.59 / -241.70	Fig. 3.98:3
86	Deposition 4	Bowl	-241.61 / -241.72	Fig. 3.98:1

in relation to the known burials; this phenomenon seems to result from the rapidity with which the interments were placed and the nature of the soil on the hillside, which leads to the extraordinarily poor preservation of artifacts, bones, and visible signs of interment. Although it is not possible to trace the layout of a tomb shaft to the burials, the relative placement of these deposits may indicate that after interment of each individual, the area above the burials may have been marked with stones or additional ceramics or both, although it is not possible to determine what length of time might have elapsed between the placement of the individual and that of the depositions.

3.3   THE WARRIOR BURIALS AT GESHER

3.3.1   Description of the Burials

Seven of the burials at Gesher (Graves 2, 12–14, 18–19, and 22) included metal weapons among the associated grave goods, and represent an interment type generally characterized as warrior burials. While most studies tend to concentrate on the typology and chronology of the weapons found in these burials (Maxwell-Hyslop 1949; Yadin 1963; Oren 1971; Dever 1975; Gerstenblith 1983; Miron 1992: 58–67), only seldom is consideration given to the customs associated with the warrior burials themselves (Oren 1971; Philip 1995b). The seven undisturbed single warrior burials found at Gesher, preserved mostly intact and representing almost a third of interments excavated in the cemetery, present the possibility of examining this custom in more detail.[9] As a detailed description of the graves was provided above, only the relevant data pertaining to the skeletons and the associated grave goods is presented here.

GRAVE 2: This individual was oriented east–west, with the head in the east and the legs in the west. The skeleton was lying in a flexed position on its right side, facing north. A bronze duckbill axe, a bowl, and remains of animal bones were found near the head. A large jar and a bronze spearhead were found close to the legs.

GRAVE 12: The skeleton was oriented east–west, lying on the right side in a flexed position, with the face and knees to the north. A jar and a bronze duckbill axe were found near the head.

GRAVE 13: This burial was oriented east–west, the skeleton lying in a flexed position, facing north, with the head in the east and the legs in the west. The grave goods included a bronze duckbill axe located near the head and a bronze spearhead under the arms. Near the chest, to the north, were found a painted jar and a bowl; faunal remains were unearthed near the bowl.

GRAVE 14: This burial was oriented south–north, the body lying in a flexed position, with the head in the south and the legs in the north. Adjacent to the skull in the south, a jar and a bowl with four knobs were found with a bronze axe inside the bowl. On the stone construction associated with the burial, three additional vessels were unearthed: a small juglet, a large juglet and a bowl.

GRAVE 18: This individual was oriented south–north, lying flexed on the right side, with the head to the south. A jar and a painted jug were found near the individual's feet and a bronze spearhead was found to the southeast of the head; a third vessel, an open bowl, was found placed upside down at the lowest level of the stones of the associated wall, outside the burial chamber.

GRAVE 19: This burial was oriented south–north, lying flexed on the right side, with the head to the south and the face and knees to the east. The grave goods included a two-handled store jar located near the lower legs and feet; a spearhead was found at the base of the jar. A carinated bowl was found some distance to the east of the legs and a hemispheric bowl and a large open bowl were found in front of the individual's arms and chest.

GRAVE 22: This individual was oriented south–north, lying in a flexed position on the left side, with the head to the south. The only grave goods associated with the body was a bronze spearhead found lying under the right lower arm.

3.3.2   Discussion

All of the warrior burials possess similar characteristics: despite differences in tomb construction (different shaft constructions at Gesher; a variety of other tomb styles has been attested at other sites, such as Baghouz [du Mesnil du Buisson 1948], Kabri [Gershuny 1989], and Rehov [Yogev 1985]), they are all primary burials in a flexed position. The associated grave goods found with the burials included a combination of different artifact types (Table 3.2) but, in general, the variety of items placed in the tombs was quite limited. The standard assemblage seems to have included an axe, a spearhead, a jar/jug, and a bowl. Sometimes one or another of the items was lacking and sometimes one was added, but these variations do not alter the composition of the basic paraphernalia of the deceased.

In general, offerings in the warrior tombs at Gesher consisted of the following items:

CLOSED VESSELS: Seven closed vessels – either jars or jugs – were discovered in the seven graves. It should be noted, however, that two closed vessels were found with Grave 18 and no ceramics at all were discovered in association with Grave 22, so there is not a direct one-to-one correlation of jars/jugs with the burials. Significantly, unlike warrior burials found at other sites, no juglets at all were discovered in association with the warrior burials at Gesher.[10] It is probable that the jars/jugs may have contained beer (Maeir and Garfinkel 1992; Gates 1988: 69–73; also see discussion in Chapter 9).

BOWLS: A total of seven bowls was found with the burials. At Baghouz some of the bowls were made of wood. Four of the graves contained one bowl, while three bowls were found with Grave 19 and none at all with Graves 12 and 22. The bowl found in Grave 14 at Gesher was a large open form, with knobbed decoration. Similar bowls found in association with warrior burials are attested in Tomb 990 at Kabri (Gershuny 1989: 14, fig. 14), Tomb 1 at Ginosar (Epstein 1974, fig. 7:3; fig. 15) and Level 3 of Tomb IV at Tell Sukas (Thrane 1978: 25–26, figs. 32–33, 78, 86).

AXES: Four axes, three duckbill and one socket axe, were found in four separate burials (Graves 2, 12–14); Graves 18, 19 and 22, however, did not have an axe.

TABLE 3.2 Weapons and ceramics found in association with the warrior burials at Gesher with comparative data from warrior burials excavated at Baghouz, Rehov, and Kabri.

Tomb	Jar/Jug	Bowl	Axe	Spearhead	Dagger	Juglet
Gesher Grave 2	1	1	1	1	–	–
Gesher Grave 12	1	–	1	–	–	–
Gesher Grave 13	1	1	1	1	–	–
Gesher Grave 14	1	1	1	–	–	–
Gesher Grave 18	2	1	–	1	–	–
Gesher Grave 19	1	3	–	1	–	–
Gesher Grave 22	–	–	–	1	–	–
No of items	7	7	4	5	0	0
Baghouz Z-67	1	1	1	1	–	–
Baghouz Z-95	1	1	–	3	–	–
Baghouz Z-121	1	1	1	1	–	–
Baghouz Z-122	1	1	2	1	1	–
Baghouz Z-123	1	1	2	1	–	–
Baghouz Z-141	1	1	2	1	–	–
Baghouz Z-143	1	1	1	1	–	–
Rehov 2	1	1	–	2	–	–
Kabri T. 990	2	1	1	–	1	2

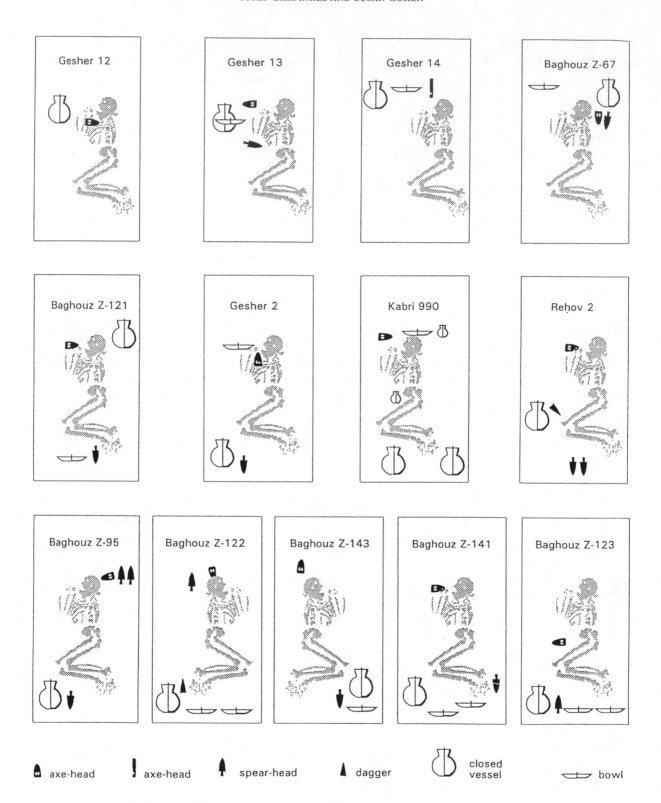

FIG 3.99 *Position of offerings in relation to the skeleton in the warrior burials.*

SPEARHEADS: Five spearheads were excavated from the seven burials; the individuals in Graves 12 and 14 were buried without a spearhead.

DAGGERS: No daggers were recovered from any of the warrior burials at Gesher. Daggers have been found in other warrior burial contexts at Baghouz Z-122 (du Mesnil du Buisson 1948) and Kabri Tomb 990 (Gershuny 1989).

The position of the offerings in the tomb in relation to the skeleton varied slightly from grave to grave (fig. 3.99).

POSITION OF AXE: Out of the four axes discovered in the various graves, the three duckbill axes were placed close to the head of the deceased, and the socket axe was found in a bowl located near the head and chest of the individual. Because of the position of the axes near the head, it is suggested that the individual was grasping the handle of the axe.

POSITION OF THE SPEARHEAD: Out of the five spearheads discovered in the graves, two were found near the legs and feet of the corpse, one close to the head, and two close to the arms and hands. There is no single distinct pattern; it may be that the shaft of the spear could be grasped in such a way that the spearhead ended up in different positions in the graves.

POSITION OF JAR/JUG: Out of seven jars or jugs discovered in the graves, four were placed near the legs or feet and three were near the head.

POSITION OF BOWL: Of the seven bowls excavated with the burials, one was located near the legs, two were near the head, three were near the chest and middle of the body, and one was placed outside the stone construction blocking the grave.

While the grave sample is too small to support any definite conclusion, it may be noted that the percentage of warrior burials among the interments excavated from the cemetery at Gesher is thirty percent, which is almost a third of the total number of burials. It is known that children were buried in storage jars under the floors of the houses in this period, and no child's grave has been found at Gesher. The cemeteries thus reflect the composition of the adult community. Half of the interments are female and, consequently, a quarter

of the population indicates that every second male was a warrior. This percentage is rather high and could not represent a segregated class of warriors; it rather suggests that most of the adult population carried arms.

Despite the fact that the Bronze Age objects, in general, and bronze weapons, in particular, were precious items, they were, nevertheless, buried with their owners. This suggests that the weapons were personal possessions of the warrior and were not controlled by central authority or stored together in a community arsenal. Weapons were considered personal belongings. At the warrior's death, they were not bequeathed but were buried with him. Costly weapons thus went out of circulation. The society was able to produce new weapons, since the copper and tin required for the production of bronze were available.

It should be noted that burials associated with weapons as grave goods were common in the southern Levant in the earlier period – the Middle Bronze Age I, ca. 2300–2000 BCE (Philip 1995b). Many Middle Bronze I graves are characterized by individual burials in a flexed position and grave offerings consisting of ceramic vessels and weapons, usually daggers and javelins. In rare cases, axes of fenestrated eye-type were also included, as reported from Neve-Eytan, Megiddo, and Ma'abarot (Miron 1992: 53). Such burials have been reported in almost every cemetery of the period, including 'Enan (Eisenberg 1985), Beth Shan (Oren 1973: 170–81), Dhahr Mirzbaneh (Lapp 1966: fig. 24), Jericho (Kenyon 1960: 188–90), Lachish (Tufnell 1958: pls. 14, 21), and Tell el-Ajjul (Petrie 1932: pls. 9–13). It appears that the custom of burying warriors individually with weapons crystallized in the last third of the third millennium BCE in the Levant, and from the evidence provided by the Gesher cemetery it may be suggested that these customs may have continued through the MB I–MB IIA transition period into the early phases of MB IIA.

3.4 THE GRAVE ARCHITECTURE

As noted above, the burials were dug into soft sediment and blocked immediately after the burial with the same sediment that had been removed while

TABLE 3.3 Distribution of stones in the Gesher graves.

GRAVE	NO STONES	ONE–TWO STONES	ELONGATED ROW	THICK CONSTRUCTION
G-1			+	
G-2				+
G-3		+		
G-4 Upper			+	
G-4 Lower	?			
G-5				+
G-6			?	
G-7	?			
G-8	?			
G-9		+		
G-10		?		
G-11			+	
G-12			+	
G-13	?			
G-14				+
G-15	?			
G-16				
G-17		+		
G-18				+
G-19		+		
G-20				
G-21				
G-22	?			
G-23				+
Total:	6	5	5	5

digging the graves. Because of this, it was not possible to determine the exact outlines of the burial or burial chamber. The size of the burial chamber may be deduced from the distance between the stones and the skeleton and grave goods. In cases where the skeleton and the offerings were very close to the stones, such as Graves 11, 12, 18 and 23, this may indicate a small or narrow burial chamber. In other burials, however, such as Graves 2, 5, 14, and 17, the skeletons and offerings are nearly a meter away from the blocking construction, which suggests a larger burial chamber.

The stone construction unearthed near most of the skeletons provides the only indication regarding the shape and type of the shaft and the construction of the grave (Table 3.3).

NO STONES: In six graves no stones were found. This situation may reflect a simple pit burial with no shaft or chamber. It is also possible that the stones were eroded away from the slope of the hill or destroyed by modern road constructions and not located during the excavations.

ONE–TWO STONES: In five graves only one or two stones were found. In the case of a rounded burial shaft, only one or two stones would be needed to block the entrance from the shaft to the burial chamber. Other examples of a rounded burial shaft blocked by one or two stones are attested at Jericho (Kenyon 1960: fig. 178; Kenyon 1965: figs. 193, 211, 221, 223), Kh. Kufin (Smith 1962: pl. V), Tell Fara South (Price-Williams 1977: fig. 69), and Efrata (Gonen 2001: fig. 22). The five graves with one or two stones at Gesher (Graves 3, 9, 10, 17, and 19) may have had a rounded shaft.

ELONGATED ROW: In five graves, one row of stones was found, located anywhere from a few centimeters to nearly a meter away from the skeleton. A row of stones suggests a rectangular shaft, as in this case one or two stones would not suffice to block the entrance from the shaft to the burial chamber. Rather, a row of stones, placed the length of the shaft, would have been needed to fully block the entrance. Such constructions were reported from the Tel Aviv cemetery (Kaplan 1959), Tell Fara South (Price-Williams 1977: figs. 25, 72), Barqai (Gophna and Sussman 1969: fig. 2), Efrata (Gonen 2001: fig. 19), and Jericho (Kenyon 1965: figs. 132, 211, 246). The five graves at Gesher with one row of stones (Graves 1, 4A, 11, 12, and possibly 6) may have had a more rectangular shaped shaft.

THICK CONSTRUCTION: In five graves (Graves 2, 5, 14, 18, and 23), two adjacent rows, or a square or rectangular massive construction of stone was found. In these cases it seems that the stones blocked the entire lower part of the shaft and not just the entrance to the burial chamber. The size and shape of these constructions indicate that the shaft may have had a square shape. The strategy in this case would have been not to block just the entrance from the shaft to the burial chamber, but to use stones to block the entire lower part of the shaft. Similar examples are attested at Jericho (Kenyon 1965: figs. 138, 175, 193, 223) and in the rock-cut shaft graves of Tell Fara South (Price-Williams 1977: fig. 34).

3.5. DISCUSSION

From the interments excavated in the cemetery, it is possible to discuss aspects of the burial process, described in more detail below, in connection with the deposition of the offerings, and subsequent inferences that may be made concerning the social order of the community buried at Gesher.

1. Preparing the body.
   The primary burials were all lying in a flexed position (see, for example, figs. 3.46, 3.55).[11] As the corpse would have become stiff about 10 hours after death and rigor mortis would have lasted at least three days, placing the body in a flexed position had to take place either immediately after death or a few days later.

2. Transferring the corpse to the cemetery.
   Gesher is not located near any known MB IIA settlement. If there was a nearby dwelling site, it must have been a small village that is now completely covered under later alluvial deposits or destroyed by modern activities in the area. Another possibility is that Gesher was used by a pastoral group that used the area seasonally.

3. Digging the grave.
   Unlike many other Middle Bronze Age cemeteries that were cut into hard rock, the graves at Gesher were cut in the soft local sediment. This seems to have been a deliberate choice, as the limestone mountains of Galilee are located less then two to three km to the west. Digging such a shaft grave in the softer sediment could be achieved in a day's work by a group of three to four people.

4. Placing the body in the grave.
   The body would have been taken down the shaft and placed in the burial chamber.

5. Laying out the body in the burial chamber
   Placing the body with the head to the east and the legs to the west was the more common custom; in three cases, however, the body was oriented with the head to the south. In general, the deceased was placed facing the entrance of the grave (e.g., fig. 3.92). Additionally, it seems that the individual was put into the grave with some clothing, as indicated by the toggle pin unearthed in Grave 5.

6. Funerary equipment.
   Unlike other Middle Bronze Age burials in which beds in funerary contexts were interred with the deceased, such as at Baghouz (du Mesnil du Buisson 1948) and Jericho (Kenyon 1960; 1965), there is no evidence of mortuary furniture at Gesher. In a few cases, however, as discussed above, the heads of the deceased were placed on flat medium-sized stones, as if they served as pillows, which might be a symbolic representation of a bed.

7. Providing for the deceased.
   Various types of food and offerings were placed

TABLE 3.4 Offerings found in association with each interment.

GRAVE	SHALLOW BOWL	DEEP BOWL	JUGLET	BOTTLE	JUG	JAR	AXE	SPEARHEAD	TOGGLE PIN	WORKED BONE	TOTAL ITEMS	ANIMAL BONES
G-1	1					1					2	
G-2	1					1	1	1			4	+
G-3		1									1	
G-4A	2	1								1	4	
G-4B	1				1	1					3	+
G-5	1								1		2	
G-6												
G-7			1		1					1	3	
G-8	1				1	1					3	
G-9	1	2				1					4	
G-10	2	2			2	1					7	+
G-11						1					1	
G-12						1	1				2	
G-13	1					1	1	1			4	+
G-14	2		2		1	1					6	
G-15	3					1					4	
G-16		1			1	1					3	
G-17	1	1				2					4	
G-18	1				1	1		1			4	
G-19	1	2				1		1			5	
G-20	1					1					2	
G-21	1					1					2	+
G-22								1			1	
G-23	1					1					2	+
Total	22	10	3		8	18	4	5	1	2	73	6

in the grave, most probably consisting of meat, beer, and probably also bread and cooked foods. The animal bones found near several of the open bowls indicate meat offerings (see Chapter 10), and other foods would have been placed in other containers. In addition, the perforated bone discovered inside the jar in Grave 7 clearly indicates the presence of beer (see Chapter 9). Thus, the ceramics found in association with the burials were containers for this food; they were not deposited in the graves simply because of their own merit, and these offerings may indicate some sort of belief in an afterlife. The food may have been supplies for the journey between the world of the living and the world of the dead; it

is also possible that the food might stem from a funerary banquet held for the deceased (Baker 2003).

8. Providing symbols of status or other social indications.

The bronze weapons found with seven of the interments fit the pattern of "warrior burials." Other than these weapons, the one toggle pin, and one perforated bone near the body of Grave 4A, no artifacts indicative of status were found at Gesher. No beads or jewelry were found in any of the burials. The burial of bronze weapons and the toggle pin with the deceased resulted in the removal of rather expensive luxury goods from circulation within the community. While these offerings may have been part of a belief in an afterlife, their placement in the graves also has direct implications for the living members of the population, as the possession of these goods also symbolizes richness (social importance) of certain families or individuals within the community.

9. Closing the chamber.

When the placement of the body and offerings was concluded, the entrance to the chamber was blocked by local stones, most probably gathered in the nearby Wadi Nahal.

10. Placing additional offerings.

Sometimes additional offerings were placed on top of the stones, such as the bowl placed outside the stone construction of Grave 18, or the item on the stones associated with Grave 14.

11. Blocking the shaft.

The shaft was filled in, apparently with the same sediment removed while digging the grave.

12. Marking the grave.

There is no clear evidence indicating that the grave spot was marked on the surface, such as by stones, a heap of earth, or organic remains. It is possible that the four depositions without skeletal remains may be representative of post-interment marking. In addition, the fact that Grave 10 was reopened also indicates that there was some means of identifying the location of earlier burials.

The mortuary offerings of both food and luxury goods indicate aspects relating to the social order and level of stratification of the Gesher community. In the graves at Gesher, the number of offerings usually did not exceed four to an individual, although the total number varies from grave to grave (Table 3.4). In all cases, the deceased was interred with at least one ceramic object.[12]

It can be suggested that all individuals, regardless of status, were buried with basic provisions; either, as suggested above, as sustenance for the afterlife or as part of the funerary banquet. The additional items, including the bronzes or any further ceramics, may then be indicative of some level of the wealth or status of the deceased, such as the warrior burials discussed above. In general, the variation between graves is slight. Unlike rich tombs uncovered in various Middle and Late Bronze sites, at Gesher the overall picture is rather simple and the cemetery reflects a rather egalitarian society.[13]

NOTES

1 During the 2002–2004 excavations, the numbering of graves was started again at 1 with the identification and excavation of the first interment, resulting in Burials 1–8; all previous publications regarding the 2002–2004 excavations refer to this numbering system (Cohen 2003a; 2003b; 2004a; 2004b; 2005). For the compilation of the final excavation report, Burials 1–8 from the 2002–2004 season were changed to Graves 16–23 in order to present a synthesized analysis of all the data from the cemetery.

2 Note that three of the interments, Graves 3, 16, and 20 were secondary burials.

3 Neither form had any diagnostic sherds preserved; therefore, these two vessels were not drawn and do not appear on the illustrations of associated material culture accompanying Grave 17.

4 The jar was so badly broken and deteriorated that it proved impossible to restore.

5 Grave 18 is the exception to this pattern; the structure that presumably blocked the entrance to the burial chamber was located at the feet of the individual.

6 In the preliminary publication of this material (Cohen 2003b), it was suggested that the position of Grave 16 (discussed as Burial 1 in the initial publication) may have resulted from post-depositional slide from erosion on the hillside. This suggestion has since been discounted, as there is no evidence for this type of movement, and Grave 16 is consistent with the other secondary burials found at the site.

7 The bones missing from the secondary depositions are generally the smaller bones, such as those from the hands and feet, or those which would not usually preserve well. For further discussion, see Chapter 4.

8 Similar deposits of pottery not associated with skeletal remains are attested at the cemetery at Dhahrat el-Humraiya (Ory 1948: fig. 2).

9 For a more detailed discussion regarding the nature of the warrior burials at other comparative sites, such as Baghouz, Kabri, and Rehov, see Garfinkel 2001.

10 This, however, is in keeping with the relatively small number of juglets found at the site overall (see Chapter 5).

11 Ilan (1996: 255–58) has suggested that the contracted position of the skeleton simulated the fetus, and the shaft tomb simulated the womb.

12 Grave 22, where the only grave good was a bronze spearhead, is an exception to this, as no ceramics were uncovered in relation to this burial; as noted previously, this burial was severely disturbed by the road cut and subsequent erosion, and in all probability there were ceramics associated with the interment that did not survive until excavation.

13 It is also important to note that this examination of social elements reflected in the cemetery at Gesher is restricted to an adult population only. No infant or child burial has been uncovered at the site, and there is no evidence pertaining to status or treatment of this segment of the population.

Chapter 4

The Skeletons

by Wiesław Więckowski

4.1 INTRODUCTION

The excavations at Gesher yielded the remains of twenty-one individuals, of which eight are presented here (Table 4.1). The remains from the 1986–1987 seasons were excavated and transferred to Tel Aviv for further analysis. Before this could take place, however, these remains were sent for re-burial, in keeping with the law regarding the treatment of human remains; as such, they were never properly analyzed and are not included in this report. The eight individuals uncovered during the 2002–2004 seasons of excavation were excavated with the assistance of a physical anthropologist present in the field and were analyzed *in situ*. This proved to be the only way to obtain any information regarding the skeletons, since the state of preservation of the bones was far from good.

The nature of the soil in which the individuals were deposited caused substantial loss in bone substance, resulting in the extreme fragility and fragmentary preservation of the skeletons. It is also clear that the collapsing roofs of the burial chambers played an additional significant role in the fragmentation of the bones, causing both breakage and post mortem deformations.

This state of preservation had inevitable influence on and implications for both sex and age at death estimations based on the morphological analysis of diagnostic regions of the human skeleton, discussed further below. No measurements of the cranium or the postcranial skeleton could be obtained, not only due to fragmentary preservation, but also because of post mortem deformation of the bones, as well as partial dissolving of the bone substance. Most of the fragile parts of the skeletons and almost all of the joint areas were either completely dissolved or in an extremely poor state of preservation; they could be observed only at the time of their exposure during the actual excavation.

4.2 METHODOLOGY

The age at death of an individual can be determined with varying degrees of success depending on the period of life reached. The estimation is based on the evaluation of various aspects of the skeletal development, tooth eruption, and tooth wear during life (Piontek 1999; Bass 1995). For age estimations at Gesher, due to the specific nature of the preservation, the observation of the dentition, morphological and developmental traits of

TABLE 4.1 *Skeletons excavated in the 2002–2004 seasons at Gesher.*

BURIAL NUMBER	BURIAL CHARACTER	STATE OF PRESERVATION	POSITION	SEX	AGE	PATHOLOGIES
G-16	secondary	poor	NA	male	*adultus*, early *maturus*	dental calculuus on lower incisors
G-17	primary	good–poor	flexed, on right side, head to E	female	*juvenis*	changes on the long bone surface
G-18	primary	extremely poor	flexed, on the right side, head to S	male	*adultus/maturus*	changes on the tibia's shaft
G-19	primary	good	flexed, on the right side, head to S	male	*adultus*	caries on M2
G-20	secondary	good/poor	NA	male	*adultus, adultus/ maturus*	?
G-21	primary	extremely poor	flexed, on the right side, head to E	female (?)	*adult*	?
G-22	primary	extremely poor	unknown	male (?)	?	?
G-23	primary	good	flexed, on the left side, head to E	male	*adultus*	?

the long bones, and cranial features (especially the cranial sutures and the degree of their closure – *obliteration*) were used. Most of the information was obtained in the field. The age is approximated into the following segments: *infant* (until the age of 14), *juvenis* (between 14 and 21), *adultus* (between 21 and 35), *maturus* (between 35 and 55), and *senilis* (55 and over).

The assessment of sex was based on purely morphological characteristics of the diagnostic parts of the skeletons. Due to the state of preservation, almost no pelvic bones were present (Grave 23 is an exception), forcing the estimated sex to be based on other features, such as cranial features (e.g., the exposure of the *processus mastoideus* or the morphology of the frontal bone), and/or some features on the long bones (especially the morphology of the proximal end of the femur), as well as overall morphology (Piontek 1999; Bass 1995). All assessments were made following the exposure of the skeletons in the field, since even the use of

PVA to conserve the bones of the most distinctive regions was not successful. Because of the impossibility of obtaining cranial measurements, due to the fragmentary nature of the interments and the *post mortem* deformations, it was impossible to compare the morphometric characteristics of the skeletons with other sites from the same or a similar time range; this problem also applied to the estimation of stature.

4.3   THE BURIALS — DESCRIPTION OF THE REMAINS

Grave 16

This burial contained only fragments of the cranium and some long bones that were lying without any anatomical order. The nature of the deposit indicates that it was a secondary burial. The bones were packed together, with the cranium lying on the long bones, and the configuration of the bones showed some typical features that are usually present when a skeleton has been uncovered and re-interred. Only the main long bones were present (i.e., a few pieces of the femora, tibiae, humeri, and possibly other bones of the lower arm and lower leg), which were easy to collect, as well as the cranium, which had been placed on the top of the other bones.

BONES PRESENT: *cranium* – pieces of the cranial vault (i.e., pieces of the frontal, parietal, occipital and temporal bones), small fragments of the face bones, and teeth; *post-cranial skeleton* – fragments of the shafts of the long bones from the upper and lower extremities.

EXAMINATION: teeth – eight fragments: incisor, two canines, two premolars, one root fragment of a premolar, two molars (second upper left and right). The incisor's crown was worn almost to half of its height; the cusps of the other teeth were also worn. The morphology of the preserved fragments, primarily from the long bones and the diagnostic features on the cranium, shows that the person was male. The estimated age, based on fragments of fused *sutura sagittalis* and tooth wear, is *adultus/maturus*, over 35 years old.

Grave 17

This burial consisted of the remains of a skeleton in primary deposition. The body was laid on the right side, with the head to the southeast and flexed. While almost all anatomical regions of the skeleton were present, they were in a very poor state of preservation. Some of the bones had apparently dissolved completely and were not present, as well as almost all joint areas.

BONES PRESENT: *cranium* – fragments of the cranial vault (parietal, temporal, and occipital bones fragments); the face was not preserved, except for the mandible and some teeth with small fragments of the upper jawbones; *post-cranial skeleton* – fragments of the cervical vertebrae, left clavicle, some fragments of the rib bodies, scapula, upper and lower arm bones (humeri, ulnae, radii), possibly some fragments of the metacarpal bones, as well as phalanges; traces of the innominate bones, both femora and the left tibia were also present.

EXAMINATION: teeth – one upper incisor, one lower incisor and two lower left molars, slightly worn (just on the very top of the cusps). The morphology of the preserved parts of the cranium (especially the occipital part and mandible), as well as the delicate structure of the post-cranial bones suggest that the sex of the deceased was possibly female. The age is estimated as *juvenis*, between 16 and 20 years.

Grave 18

This was an extremely poorly preserved skeleton, laid on the right side, with the head to the south in a flexed position.

BONES PRESENT: *cranium* – very small pieces of the cranial vault and the facial part were present, as well as some teeth; *post-cranial skeleton* – a few fragments of the humerus shaft, a few fragments of the lower arm bones (ulna and radius), left femur and tibia, right tibia. The rest of the skeleton was dissolved completely. Some pathological changes of the bone surface, which may have been a result of some kind of inflammation, were observed on one tibia fragment.

EXAMINATION: teeth – four fragments of two upper and one lower incisors, two crown fragments of canines, two lower right premolars. All were worn, uncovering the inner parts of the teeth. Although the extremely poor state of preservation limited the information that could be obtained, the morphology of the femur shaft suggests that the individual was male. The age, which could be estimated only on the teeth wear, was *adultus/maturus*, possibly over 40.

Grave 19

This was a comparatively well-preserved skeleton, laid on the right side, with the head to the south in a flexed position.

BONES PRESENT: *cranium* – when uncovered, the cranium was almost intact, although post-mortal deformation, due to post-depositional processes, made taking measurements impossible. All of the cranial vault bones were present (fig. 4.1), as well as most of the facial bones (with the exception of

FIG. 4.1　*View of the cranium from Grave 19.*

parts of the upper jawbones). Almost the entire set of teeth was present; *post-cranial skeleton* – a few pieces of the cervical vertebrae (atlas), parts of the clavicle, a few fragments of ribs, left humerus, parts of the left ulna and radius shafts, a few pieces of carpal bones, parts of metacarpals and phalanges, large parts of the innominate bones (pelvis), an almost intact femur, right patella, and proximal fragments of the tibiae and fibulae, and poorly preserved remains of the right tarsals, metatarsals, and phalanges.

EXAMINATION: teeth – all teeth were present, although the lower left canine and premolars were preserved only as roots in the fragment of the mandible body. Some cavity changes could be observed on the upper left canine and premolars. The diagnostic parts of the cranium (e.g., the orbital part of the frontal bone, mastoid process, chin region of the mandible), as well as the morphology of the post-cranial skeleton clearly mark the individual as male. The age, estimated from tooth wear and fusion of the suturae, was *adultus*, around 30 years, or possibly slightly older.

Grave 20

This was clearly a secondary deposit, as indicated by the disarticulation and nature of deposition of the bones. The skull was placed on top of the pile of long bones and other parts of the skeleton, with the mandible in between; most of the bones of Burial 20 were present, with only small bones from hands and feet absent.

BONES PRESENT: *cranium* – most of the neurocranium was present, although in many pieces. The face was heavily damaged; the mandible was almost intact but in two separate pieces; *post-cranial skeleton* – both femora and tibiae, right humerus (in several fragments), left ulna, poorly preserved pieces of pelvis and scapula; a few rib fragments were deposited in the upper layer, and several rib fragments, clavicle, pieces of the upper and lower arm bones were found in the lower layer of the pile. The right side of the mandible (with teeth) was deposited in the lower layer and the left side of the mandible (with teeth) in the upper one.

EXAMINATION: distinctive parts of the skull (*pro-*

cessus mastoideus, os occipitalis) and mandible (*prouberantia mentalis*), as well as the morphology of the postcranial skeleton show that it belonged to a male individual, *adultus* or *adultus/maturus*.

Grave 21

This skeleton was extremely poorly preserved. The bones were almost completely dissolved, and were visible only while *in situ*. Despite this fact, it was possible to identify almost the entire skeleton.

Bones present: *cranium* – pieces of the neurocranium, traces of the face (one tooth present); *post-cranial skeleton* – left humerus, left ulna and radius (pieces of the shafts), some rib fragments, pieces of the clavicle and possibly of the scapula, very poorly preserved fragments of the pelvis, both femora. The left tibia was in the correct anatomical position, the right was moved out of position; some pieces of the metatarsals and phalanges were also present. No traces of the back bone were found.

Examination: overall dimensions and morphology of the bones suggest that this was the interment of a female individual, *adultus*.

Grave 22

This was an extremely poorly preserved burial; some of the remains may have been partially removed by the road cut. In addition to the main portion of the skeleton, some leg bones were collected from the eroded area below the burial along the edge of the cut. These bone fragments were completely desiccated and extremely poorly preserved and were discarded.

Bones present: *cranium* – no traces of the cranium were found within this burial; *post-cranial skeleton* – some parts of the rib cage (both left and right), part of the right radius, part of the left arm bone, the upper part of the sacrum, a few pieces of the pelvis, shafts of both femora, and some very small chips of the shafts of some long bones were present from this individual.

Examination: The state of preservation of the skeleton precluded definitive analysis regarding the sex and/or age of the individual. There are, however, some observations that are worth men-

tioning. First of all, this burial had a spearhead as a grave good, which suggests that it belonged to a male individual. This would correspond well with the characteristics of the bones from the eroded part of the burial, as some parts of the back of the femur shafts showed male features. The absence of most of the skeleton, including the skull, could suggest that the individual was quite young, as the bones of young individuals dissolve and erode easier than those of adults. None of this evidence, however, is definitive, and the sex and age of the individual remain speculative.

Grave 23

This burial was, comparatively speaking, very well preserved. The body was laid in a flexed position on the left side, with the head to the east.

Bones present: The *cranium* was smashed and disarticulated under the pressure of the soil. The neurocranium was present in several fairly large pieces, including the almost entirely preserved frontal lobe (fig 4.2). The face was preserved only partially, with the mandible broken in the middle; *post-cranial skeleton* – this individual was almost entirely preserved. Under the skull were a few almost completely preserved upper cervical vertebrae, including the atlas and axis. The thoracic part of the back bone was rather poorly preserved, but there were some traces of the vertebrae, especially in the upper part. The lumbar vertebrae were clearly visible, as well as the sacrum. Both of the clavicles were present, with the right one almost intact; also preserved was the right scapula and a number of rib fragments, including a nicely preserved right first rib. Also present was the right humerus (lacking parts of the shaft and distal fragments), the proximal part of the right ulna, and the middle part of the right radius shaft. The left arm was absent, except for a few fragments of the humerus shaft and carpals; the metacarpals and phalanges of the left hand were found under the cranium. The pelvis was amazingly well preserved and was found in its almost correct anatomical position (fig. 4.3). Only the proximal part of the left femur was preserved, with the head still in the acetabulum. The shaft of the right femur was preserved, as well

Fig. 4.2   *Detail of the cranium and frontal lobe from Grave 23.*

Fig. 4.3   *Detail of the pelvis from Grave 23.*

as the distal end. The lower parts of the legs were less well preserved; no traces of the left tibia and fibula remained, except a few chips of the shafts, and the right tibia was preserved only in the distal part. The right foot, however, was almost entirely present, with tarsals, metatarsals and phalanges in their anatomical position. The left foot was less well preserved, as only some of the bones were present.

EXAMINATION: The state of preservation allowed for the examination of many characteristics and distinctive areas of the skeleton. Details of the pelvis morphology, as well as of the cranium, show that it was most likely a male individual, *adultus*, in his late thirties.

4.4   PATHOLOGIES

The state of the bone preservation made the observation of pathologies almost impossible. Only a few features could be described as pathologies:

- the presence of moderately accumulated dental calculus on the side of the lower incisors from Grave 16.
- three fragments of the long bones from Grave 17 showed changes in the surface structure, although it is not clear if their character was of pathological origin.

- some changes on the tibia of Grave 18 may also have resulted from pathological changes.
- the presence of caries on the surface of the molar tooth crown (M2) from Grave 19.

4.5   CONCLUSIONS

The state of preservation of the remains retrieved during the excavations in 2002–2004 could be described as poor to extremely poor and made the diagnosis of age at death and sex of the individuals difficult or even, in one case, impossible. The summary of the results of the analysis of these individuals is thus presented as follows:

GRAVE 16: secondary deposition, male, *adultus* or early *maturus* (over the age of 35).

GRAVE 17: female (?), *juvenis* (between the age of 16 and 20).

GRAVE 18: male, *adultus/maturus* (over the age of 40).

GRAVE 19: male, *adultus* (over the age of 30).

GRAVE 20: secondary deposition, male, *adultus* (between 35–40).

GRAVE 21: female, *adultus*

GRAVE 22: male (?), age uncertain

GRAVE23: male, *adultus* (late 30s).

Chapter 5

The Pottery

by Susan Cohen and Ruhama Bonfil

5.1 INTRODUCTION

A total of eighty-three ceramic vessels, most of them complete or almost complete, comprise the assemblage from the Gesher cemetery.[1] To present these data as a whole, the material has been integrated into one corpus; in this chapter, the ceramics from Gesher have been organized by type, whereas in the discussion of the burials in Chapter 3, they have been presented by burial assemblage.[2] It is hoped that the reader will first gain an impression of the objects as they were found during excavation and then be able to examine the ceramic material according to the typology identified for the overall assemblage. As one of the few early MB IIA sites located in the central Jordan Valley region and a site that incorporates characteristics of both MB I and MB IIA, Gesher provides valuable data regarding the development of material culture in this region during this time. To date, this transitional material has been noted at Tell el-Hayyat phase 5 (Falconer 1985) and in some aspects of the pre-palace phases at Aphek (Beck 2000c), but this is limited to sherd evidence only. The ceramics at Gesher, however, are whole forms, that, although MB IIA in type, also reflect earlier

influences and help to illustrate the transitional nature of the site.

The ceramics are presented in the following order: bowls (including open, carinated, S-shaped and hemispheric), juglets, bottles, jugs, and jars (Table 5.1). Each category has been further divided into sub-types, each of which is discussed separately. The goal here is to analyze similarities and parallels between the Gesher material and that from other sites, to identify differences that may result from regional variations or other considerations, and to place the assemblage from Gesher within the larger context of MB IIA pottery found in Canaan.

All of the pottery found at Gesher is characterized by the same low-quality ware, made from poorly levigated and friable material, most probably derived from clays from the local wadi. In general, the ceramics are poorly made, with thick uneven walls, and often with lopsided stances (see, for example, fig. 5.1:4–7 and fig. 5.3). The bulk of the assemblage is undecorated, but there are also eight painted pieces, two incised jars, and two forms with red slip, which amount to approximately ten percent of the corpus. No kraters, cooking pots, or lamps were found in any of the burials. While the

Table 5.1 Number and percentage of Gesher ceramics by type.

Grave	Open bowls	Carinated bowls	S-shaped bowls	Hemispheric bowls	Juglets	Bottles	Jugs	Jars	Total
G-1	1							1	2
G-2	1							1	2
G-3		1							1
G-4a	2	1							3
G-4b	1						1	1	3
G-5								1	1
G-6									0
G-7					1			1	2
G-8	1							2	3
G-9	1		2					1	4
G-10	2	2					1	2	7
G-11								1	1
G-12								1	1
G-13	1							1	2
G-14	2				2		1		5
G-15	3							4	7
G-16		1					1	1	3
G-17	1	1						3	5
G-18	1						1	1	3
G-19	1	1		1				1	4
G-20	1							1	2
G-21	1							1	2
G-22									0
G-23	1							1	2
C-1				1		1			2
C-2			1						1
C-3		1							1
C-4	1	1						1	3
Surface	4	2			1		3	1	9
Total	26	11	3	2	4	1	8	28	83
Percent (%)	31.3	13.3	3.62	2.41	4.82	1.21	9.64	·33.7	100

forms are typically MB IIA, the poor quality is less commonly attested; this may reflect the rural characteristics of the region or the transitional nature of Gesher as a site that seems to incorporate both MB I and MB IIA characteristics, and that represents a developmental pattern for the central Jordan Valley region which differs from that identified for the coastal and urban areas.

5.2　Typology and Parallels

5.2.1　Bowls

The bowls from Gesher may be divided into four basic categories: open, carinated, S-shaped, and hemispheric. Further subdivisions are identified within each category.

Open Bowls (B)

The open bowls from Gesher comprise just over thirty-one percent of the total corpus. Although differing in diameter, depth, and rim shape, they are all generally consistent with an early MB IIA repertoire. Many of them are extremely lopsided with an uneven stance; bowls with similar distortions have been found at Kabri (Kempinski et al. 2002: figs. 5.31:11; 5.32:17; 5.33:6), Tel Dan (Ilan 1996: fig. 4.77), Megiddo (Loud 1948: fig. 29:6), Ginosar (Epstein 1974: fig. 5:12–15), as well as at other sites. The predominance of forms with a flat base is consistent with the early nature of the repertoire as a whole.

The open bowls from Gesher have been divided into the following types:

Type B1: *Bowl with a flat base, rounded walls, and upright rim.* This type makes up the largest category of bowls found at Gesher. Within the category, the rim undergoes considerable variation, and the bowls in this group have been further subdivided as follows:

Type B1A1: *pronounced outward triangular rim* (fig. 5.1:1–2). Similar bowls have been found at sites such as Megiddo (Loud 1948: pl. 19:11), Munhata (Ferembach et al. 1975: fig. 10:8), Ginosar (Epstein 1974: fig. 5:13), and others.

Type B1A2: *slight outward triangular rim* (figs. 5.1:3; 5.2). There are no close parallels for this particular bowl. The exterior triangular section on this bowl is more rounded than is typical of this rim, and the upward angle of the rim is also unusual. An indentation or groove is present below the rim.

Type B1B: *inward triangular rim* (figs. 5.1:4–7; 5.3). These bowls are common in other MB IIA assemblages; the closest parallel is to the pre-palace layers at Aphek (Beck 1985: fig. 2.2).

Type B1C: *shelf rim* (figs. 5.4:1–5; 5.5). The shelf rim on these bowls sometimes has an interior triangular section (fig. 5.4:4–5). In fig. 5.4:3 the upright rim is rounded slightly at the top; an open bowl with a similar rim was found at Tell el-Hayyat (Falconer and Magness-Gardiner 1984: fig. 14:6), although with a different overall stance.

Type B1D1: *concave rim* (fig. 5.4:6–7). Both examples of this type have a concavity, or depression, in the top of the rim. A similar rim, with a deep groove, is present on a Type B2 bowl from Tell el-Hayyat (Falconer and Magness-Gardiner 1984: fig. 14:10), but in general this is not a close parallel for the examples found at Gesher.

Type B1D2: *grooved rim* (fig. 5.4:8). The example from Gesher is a very large bowl, with multiple grooves or ridges running along the top of the rim.

Type B2: *Bowl with a flat base and straight walls.* This type of bowl is less common at Gesher than the preceding category. Similar forms have been found at Tell el-Hayyat, Megiddo, Aphek, and other sites. Within this type, the bowls in this category have been subdivided into the following groups:

Type B2A: *outward triangular rim* (fig. 5.6:1–3). Straight-sided open bowls with outward triangular rims have been found at a number of other MB IIA sites. A bowl from Phase 4 at Tell el-Hayyat (Falconer and Magness-Gardiner 1984: fig. 13:4) has a less pronounced triangular section; a bowl from Golan Dolmen 14 (Epstein 1985: fig. 5:2) is also similar, although with a rounded base. Another bowl from Megiddo (Loud 1948: pl. 14:14) is smaller and has a red-painted rim.

Type B2B: *inward triangular rim* (fig. 5.6:4–5). There are no close parallels for the straight-sided bowls with inward triangular sections. The rim on fig. 5.6:4 is similar in its section and angle to several of the bowls of Type B1B (fig. 5.1:4–5). The tapering walls and the rim with small triangular section on fig. 5.6:5 have no immediate similarities to other MB IIA corpora.

Type B2C: *flat shelf rim* (fig. 5.6:6). Only one example of this type was found. A similar bowl from Phase 4 at Tell-el-Hayyat has straighter and thinner walls.

Type B3: *Bowl with a low disc base and shelf rim* (fig. 5.6:7). Only one example of this type was found at Gesher. A bowl from Megiddo, Tomb 5179, is similar in form, but is larger, burnished, and has a red-painted rim (Loud 1948: pl. 14:16).

Type B4: *Other bowl forms.* Two other large open bowls were found in the Gesher cemetery.

Type B4A: *Bowl with four knobs set around the edge* (fig. 5.6:8; 5.7–8). This bowl has a low disc base,

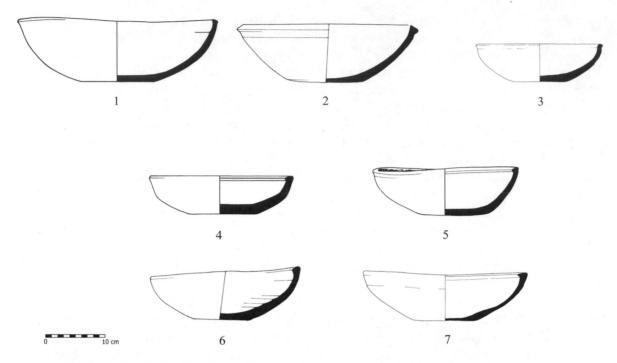

FIG. 5.1 *Open bowls from Gesher, Types B1A snd B1B.*

No.	TYPE	GR/BR #	DESCRIPTION	PARALLELS
1	B1A1	Grave 1	Flat base, rounded walls, upright rim with outward triangular section.	Megiddo T5104 (Loud 1948: pl. 19:11) Ginosar T1 (Epstein 1974: fig. 5:13) Aphek Str B Vd (Beck 2000a: fig. 8:10.2) Munhata T676 (Ferembach et al. 1975: fig. 10:8; pl. II:8)
2	B1A1	Surface	Flat base, rounded walls, upright rim with pronounced outward triangular section.	Megiddo T5104 (Loud 1948: pl. 19:11) Munhata T676 (Ferembach et al. 1975: fig. 10:8; pl. II:8)
3	B1A2	Grave 18	Flat base, rounded walls, upright rim with a small rounded outward triangular section.	
4	B1B	Grave 2	Thick flat base, rounded walls, upright rim with inward triangular section.	Aphek X20–X19 (Beck 1985: fig. 2:2)
5	B1B	Grave 4A	Flat base, rounded walls, upright rim with sharp inward triangular section.	Aphek X20–X19 (Beck 1985: fig. 2:2)
6	B1B	Surface	Flat base, rounded walls, upright rim with inward triangular section.	Aphek X20–X19 (Beck 1985: fig. 2:2)
7	B1B	Grave 17	Flat base, rounded walls, upright rim with pronounced inward triangular section.	Aphek X20–X19 (Beck 1985: fig. 2:2)

rounded walls, and an upright rim with triangular section. The four knobs or vestigial handles are set evenly spaced around the rim. This is a common form in MB IIA; these bowls are attested at other sites such as Megiddo, Aphek, and Nahariya.

Similar bowls have been found in mortuary contexts at Barqai, Ginosar, and Kabri.[3] While clearly MB IIA, this form may also continue into the later phases of the Middle Bronze Age.

TYPE B4B: *Deep bowl with tripod base* (fig. 5.6:9).

While deep bowls with three loops at the base have been found in MB IIA (Beck 2000a: fig. 8.20:11), the three-legged tripod base is otherwise unattested. A large, warped, shallow open bowl with four "legs" rather than three comes from Dolmen 14 in the Golan (Epstein 1985: fig. 5:1); with the exception of the stand, the bowl itself is quite different. The exterior triangular section on the bowl from Gesher is, however, similar to another surface find from the site, fig. 5.1:2 above.

Carinated Bowls (CB):

Carinated bowls are typical of MB IIA. However, none of the Gesher carinated forms have any red slip or burnish that is often associated with this particular form, particularly as the period progresses. Additionally, all of the carinated bowls from Gesher have relatively thick walls and flat bases, as opposed to the thinner walls and low disc bases often found on this type in early phases at other sites (Beck 2000b: fig. 10.10:1; Ilan 1996: fig. 4.106:12). The flat base as well as the lack of the gutter rim on the Gesher specimens tends to support the placement of these carinated bowls fairly early in the sequence of the development of this form.

The carinated bowls from Gesher have been divided into the following types:

TYPE CB1: *Carinated bowl with a flat base and simple rim* (fig. 5.9:1–2). On both examples of this type found at Gesher, the carination is mid-body. No close parallels are found for the simple upright rims on both forms; the everted rim of Type CB2, below, is most typically attested at other MB IIA sites.

TYPE CB2: Bowl with a flat base and everted rim.
TYPE CB2A: *lower body carination* (fig. 5.9:3–5). The three examples from Gesher are fairly small bowls; the carination on all three – quite sharp in the cases of fig. 5.9:4–5 – is set below the middle part of the vessel. A similar bowl from Megiddo (Loud 1948: pl. 14:25) has a string-cut omphalos base.

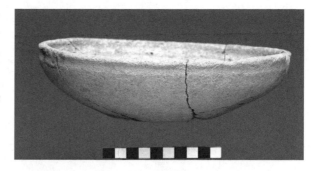

FIG. 5.2 *Open bowl with rounded triangular section and groove under the rim (fig 5.1:3).*

FIG. 5.3 *Open bowl with an inward triangular profile and uneven stance (fig. 5.1:7).*

TYPE CB2B1: *mid-body carination* (figs. 5.9:6–9; 5.10). The bowls with flat bases, everted rims, and carination at mid-body are the most common carinated bowls found at Gesher; similar bowls have been found at Megiddo (Loud 1948: pl. 14:26, pl. 28:37), Ginosar (Epstein 1974: fig. 7:5), and Hagosherim (Covello-Paran 1996: fig. 4:4-6).
TYPE CB2B2: *thin walls, wider mid-body carination* (figs. 5.9:10; 5.11). This sub-type is defined by its more delicate form than the other carinated bowls, with thinner walls and an omphalos base. Bowls with a similar delicate profile, described as cups but with straighter walls and a low disc base, have been found at Ain es-Samiyeh (Dever 1975: fig. 3:8). While parallels in Palestine are rare, similar forms are more common in Syria in the Intermediate Bronze Age and MB IIA; in the southern Levant, however, these cups or delicate carinated small bowls are found in MB IIA contexts only (Dever 1975: 34).

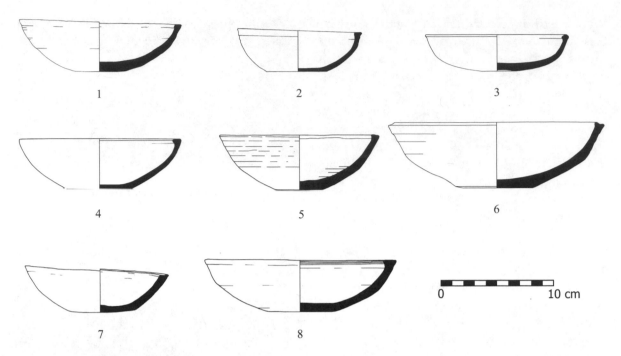

FIG. 5.4 *Open bowls from Gesher, Types B1C and B1D.*

No.	TYPE	GR/BR #	DESCRIPTION	PARALLELS
1	B1C	Deposition 4	Flat base, rounded walls, upright flat shelf rim.	Aphek (tombs by Ory; Beck 2000b: figs. 10.27.2; 10.28.2)
2	B1C	Grave 9	Flat base, rounded walls, upright flat shelf rim.	
3	B1C	Grave 10	Flat base, rounded walls, slightly rounded upright shelf rim.	Tell el-Hayyat 4 (Falconer and Magness-Gardiner 1984: fig. 14:6)
4	B1C	Grave 4B	Flat base, rounded walls, upright shelf rim with interior triangular profile.	Megiddo T3148 (Loud 1948: pl. 14:17); red wash and burnish
5	B1C	Grave 19	Flat base, rounded walls, upright shelf rim with interior triangular profile.	Aphek AXVII/AXVI (Beck 2000b: fig. 10.1.13)
6	B1D1	Grave 10	Flat base, rounded walls, with a concave rim.	Tell el-Hayyat 4 (Falconer and Magness-Gardiner 1984: fig. 14:10)
7	B1D1	Grave 23	Flat base, rounded walls, concave rim.	
8	B1D2	Grave 20	Flat base, rounded walls, grooved rim with exterior triangular section.	

FIG. 5.5 *Deep open bowl with shelf rim (fig. 5.4:5).*

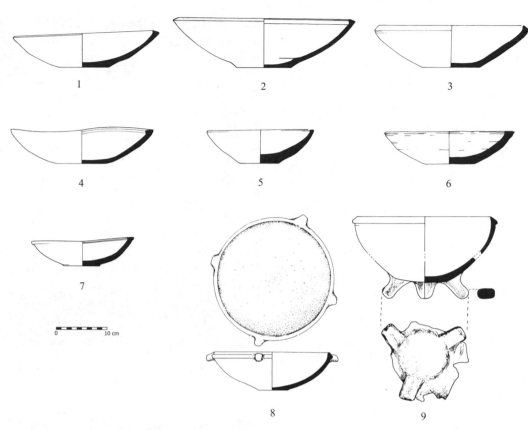

FIG. 5.6 *Open bowls from Gesher, Types B2, B3 and B4.*

No.	Type	GR/BR #	Description	Parallels
1	B2A	Grave 13	Flat base, straight walls, outward triangular rim.	Tell el-Hayyat 5 (Falconer and Magness-Gardiner 1984: fig. 13:4); Megiddo T911A (Guy 1938: pl. 28:13); Golan Dolmen 14 (Epstein 1987: fig. 5:2; this form has a rounded base)
2	B2A	Grave 14	Flat base, straight walls, outward triangular rim.	Megiddo T3143 (Loud 1948: pl. 14:14), smaller and with a red-painted rim; Ginosar T1 (Epstein 1974: fig. 5:14)
3	B2A	Surface	Flat base, straight walls, outward triangular rim.	Aphek Str B Vc (Beck 2000a: fig. 8.13.13)
4	B2B	Grave 8	Flat base, straight walls, inward triangular rim.	
5	B2B	Surface	Flat base, straight walls, inward triangular rim.	
6	B2C	Grave 21	Flat base, straight walls, flat shelf rim.	Tell el-Hayyat 4 (Falconer and Magness-Gardiner 1984: fig. 14:9)
7	B3	Grave 2	Low disc base, upright walls, shelf rim.	Megiddo T5179 (Loud 1948: pl. 14:16); bigger, with burnish, and a red painted rim.
8	B4A	Grave 14	Low disc base, inward triangular rim, with four knobs set around the edge.	Ginosar T1 (Epstein 1974: fig. 7:3); Megiddo T911A (Guy 1938: pl. 28:22); Nahariya (Ben Dor 1950: pl. X:14); Aphek X17 (Beck 1985: fig. 5:1), red-slipped and burnished; Kabri T990 (Gershuny 1989: fig. 14:1); Barqai (Gophna and Sussman 1969: fig. 7:3)
9	B4B	Grave 15	Deep bowl with tripod base and exterior triangular profile.	

S-Shaped Bowls (SB)[4]

TYPE SB1: Three S-shaped bowls were found at Gesher. S-profiled bowls make their first appearance in the early phases of MB IIA (Beck 2000b: 192); the form, however, does not appear to continue beyond the middle phases of MB IIA (Kochavi and Yadin 2002: fig. 30).

TYPE SB1A: *S-shaped bowl with simple rim* (figs. 5.12:1–2). The S-shaped bowls from Gesher have flat bases and, for the most part, simple everted rims. Fig. 5.12:2, with its high curve, has parallels at Aphek and Megiddo; the thick base and lower curve on fig. 5.12:1 is similar in shape to another bowl from Megiddo (Loud 1948: pl. 14:35), although the Megiddo bowl is burnished and has incised decoration.

TYPE SB1B: *deep S-shaped bowl with thickened rim* (fig. 5.12:3). This bowl has some similarities to deep bowls from Phase C at Tel Ifshar (Paley and Porath 1997: fig 13.2:3), although the latter has surface combing and a gutter rim.

Hemispheric Bowls (HB)

TYPE HB1: Hemispheric bowl.
The hemispheric bowl is most commonly found in early MB IIA contexts, such as the pre-palace strata at Aphek (Beck 2000b: 174, fig 10:31; Beck 2000c: 240), and does not continue into the later phases of the period (Kochavi and Yadin 2002: 196, 198, fig. 30); the presence of this form at Gesher is consistent with the early MB IIA date for the site.

TYPE HB1A: *simple rim* (fig. 5.12:4). The one hemispheric bowl with a simple rim is very thick and crudely made; a much thinner example from Phase 5 at Tell el-Hayyat (Falconer and Magness-Gardiner 1984: fig. 13:5) has a similar simple upright rim. Another bowl from Megiddo (Loud 1948: pl. 15:5) has the same thick walls and stance, although the rim differs.

TYPE HB1B: *inward triangular rim* (figs. 5.12:5; 5.13). This example is thinner and more carefully made than the other example from Gesher; an analogous form at Aphek (Beck 2000a: fig. 8.13.11) has a thicker base and straighter walls.

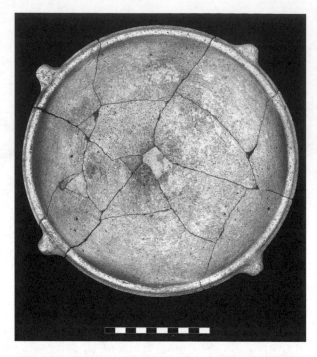

FIG. 5.7   *Open bowl with four knobs on the rim, top view (fig. 5.6:8).*

FIG. 5.8   *Open bowl with four knobs on the rim, side view (fig. 5.6:8).*

5.2.2   Juglets (JT)

Only four juglets were found in the cemetery at Gesher, amounting to just under five percent of the total corpus. This number is low when compared to other mortuary sites, especially those from later in the period, such as Efrata, where juglets made up approximately twenty-eight percent of the assemblage (Gonen 2001: 81). This, however, may reflect the change in tomb assemblages as noted by

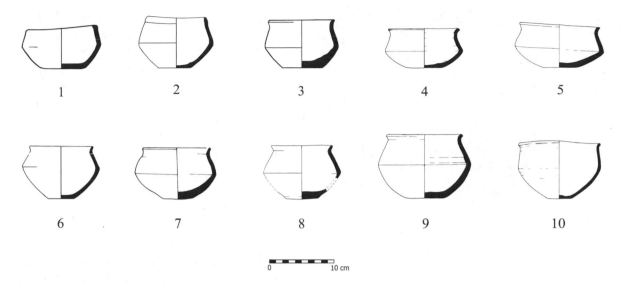

Fig. 5.9 *Carinated bowls from Gesher, Types CB1 and CB2.*

No.	Type	GR/BR #	Description	Parallels
1	CB1	Grave 3	Flat base, simple rim, carination at mid-body.	
2	CB1	Grave 10	Flat base, simple rim, carination at mid-body.	
3	CB2A	Grave 4a	Thick flat base, everted rim, carination at lower body.	Megiddo T5124 (Loud 1948: pl. 14:25)
4	CB2A	Surface	Flat base, everted rim, sharp carination at lower body.	Megiddo T5124 (Loud 1948: pl. 14:25)
5	CB2A	Grave 19	Flat base, everted rim, very sharp carination at lower body.	Megiddo T5124 (Loud 1948: pl. 14:25)
6	CB2B1	Grave 10	Flat base, everted rim, carination at mid-body.	Tell el-Hayyat 4 (Falconer and Magness-Gardiner 1984: fig. 14:14); Megiddo T5130 (Loud 1948: pl. 14:26); Megiddo T911A (Guy 1938: pl. 28:37); Golan Dolmen 13 (Epstein 1985: fig. 3:22); Golan Dolmen 14 (Epstein 1985: fig. 5:3); Ginosar T1 (Epstein 1974: fig. 7:5)
7	CB2B1	Surface	Flat base, everted rim, carination at mid-body.	Tell el-Hayyat 4 (Falconer and Magness-Gardiner 1984: fig. 14:14); Megiddo T5130 (Loud 1948: pl. 14:26); Megiddo T911A (Guy 1938: pl. 28:37); Golan Dolmen 13 (Epstein 1985: fig. 3:22); Golan Dolmen 14 (Epstein 1985: fig. 5:3); Ginosar T1 (Epstein 1974: fig. 7:5)
8	CB2B1	Grave 16	Flat base, everted rim, carination at mid-body.	Hagosherim Tomb A (Covello-Paran 1996: fig. 4:4–6)
9	CB2B1	Grave 17	Flat base, everted rim, carination at mid-body.	Hagosherim Tomb A (Covello-Paran 1996: fig. 4:4–6)
10	CB2B2	Deposition 4	Flat base, thin walls, everted rim, carination at mid-body.	Ain es-Samiyeh (Dever 1975: fig. 3:8)

Fig. 5.10. *Bowl with carination at mid-body (fig. 5.9:9).*

Fig. 5.11. *Bowl with delicate profile and carination at mid-body (fig. 5.9:10).*

Hallote (1995: 114–15) regarding the shift in focus from providing the dead with containers with food provisions early in MB IIA to an increase in luxury items being interred with the dead in the later phase of the Middle Bronze Age.

Typologically, the juglets from Gesher present characteristics consistent with the earliest ceramic phases of MB IIA; these, such as the "gutter rim" on fig. 5.14:1 and the red slip on fig. 5.14:4 (see Beck 2000b: 209–10, fig. 10:31), however, also could be present in the middle phases of the period. It should be noted that the Gesher juglets do not fit well with the general typology established for the IIA period by such "type" sites as Aphek or Megiddo. The bodies of the Gesher juglets are rounder and less elongated. In addition, the Gesher forms have wider bases and often shorter and

wider necks than is typical of the standard MB IIA repertoire (see Beck 2000b: fig. 10:31). This difference in shape is also present in the corpus of jars from the site (see below) and may be indicative of regional variations.

The juglets from Gesher may be divided into three categories:

Type JT1: *Piriform juglet* (fig. 5.14:1). Only one piriform juglet, a form common at other MB IIA mortuary sites, was found at Gesher. The example from Gesher has a gutter rim and small, flat base.

Type JT2: *Juglet with a rounded body* (fig. 5.14:2–3). Of the two forms found at Gesher, fig. 5.14:2 has a trefoil mouth, and the other (fig. 5.14:3) has a simple, slightly flared rim. Both juglets have wide, flat bases.

Type JT3: *Juglet with a bag-shaped body* (fig. 5.14:4). The one example is from the surface finds at Gesher. It has a long thin neck, a concave upright rim, with red slip and burnish. Juglets with a similar body shape were found at Megiddo (Loud 1948: pl. 19:31) and Munhata (Ferembach et al. 1975: fig. 8:1); the latter example is broken below the neck.

5.2.3   Bottles (BT)

Only one bottle has been found at Gesher.[5]

Type BT1: *Bottle with a short, wide globular body, and a flared simple rim* (fig. 5.14:5). The bottle found at Gesher is very thick and crudely made. There are no close parallels for this piece among the bottles found at other MB IIA sites in Canaan. Its wide rounded body differs from both the ovoid bottles found at Efrata (Gonen 2001: fig. 24:13), Wadi et-Tin (Vincent 1947: fig. 4:4), and Ain es-Samiyeh (Dever 1975: fig. 3:5), as well as from the squat shape of the ones from Hagosherim (Covello-Paran 1996: figs. 4:9, 9:2), although it bears a closer resemblance to the latter. The flared simple rim, however, is similar to the Hagosherim bottles in some respects, and it is possible that the bottle from Gesher may be derived from the same general Syrian influence (Covello-Paran 1996: 73).

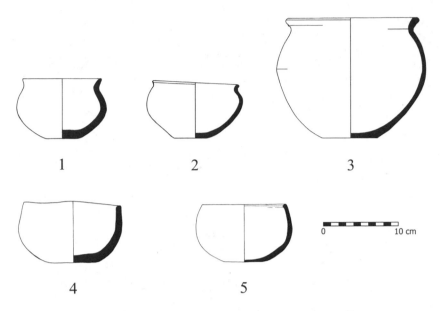

FIG. 5.12 *S-shaped and hemispheric bowls from Gesher, Types SB1 and HB1.*

No.	TYPE	GR/BR #	DESCRIPTION	PARALLELS
1	SB1A	Deposition 2	S-shaped bowl with thick flat base and simple rim.	Megiddo T5171 (Loud 1948: pl. 14:35); burnish and incised decoration.
2	SB1A	Grave 9	S-shaped bowl with flat base and simple rim.	Aphek X19-X20 (Beck 1985: fig. 2:3) Megiddo T911A1 (Guy 1938: pl. 28:35)
3	SB1B	Grave 9	Deep S-shaped bowl with flat base and thickened rim.	(Paley and Porath 1997: fig. 13.2:3); combed.
4	HB1A	Deposition 1	Hemispheric bowl with simple rim.	Tell el-Hayyat 5 (Falconer and Magness-Gardiner 1984: fig. 13:5); Megiddo T5128 (Loud 1948: pl. 15:5)
5	HB1B	Grave 19	Hemispheric bowl with inward triangular rim.	Aphek Str Vc (Beck 2000a: fig. 8.13.11)

5.2.4 *Jugs (JG)*

The jugs from Gesher fit within the general typology for MB IIA, although, again, some of the forms have wider and more rounded bodies than is attested in other assemblages. This is consistent with the rest of the repertoire from Gesher and is probably indicative of regional variation. The wide trefoil mouth found on some of the pieces, an MB IIA innovation which possibly originated in Anatolia (Amiran 1970: 61), is also consistent with an early MB IIA date. The painted pieces also support the early date for Gesher, as painted material is limited to the earliest phases of MB IIA – analogous to Aphek's pre-palace levels (Beck

FIG. 5.13 *Hemispheric bowl (fig. 5.12:5).*

2000b: 230; Cohen 2002a). Although the specific decorative patterns found in the Gesher corpus do not have exact parallels elsewhere, they are clearly

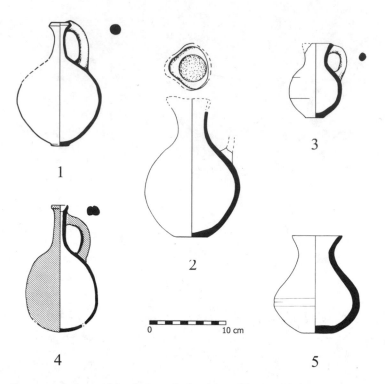

FIG. 5.14 *Juglets and bottle from Gesher, Types JT1–3 and BT1.*

No.	Type	GR/BR #	Description	Parallels
1	JT 1	Grave 7	Piriform juglet with low disc base, round handle, and concave rim.	Nahariya (Dothan 1956: pl. D:2) Hagosherim Tomb A (Covello-Paran 1996: fig. 4:10)
2	JT 2	Grave 14	Juglet with rounded body, round handle, and simple rim.	Aphek Tomb 43 (Beck 1975: fig. 14:7)
3	JT 2	Grave 14	Juglet with flat base and rounded body; rim unknown.	Munhata T676 (Ferembach et al. 1975: fig. 10:7)
4	JT 3	Surface	Red-slipped juglet with a bag-shaped body, figure-eight handle and simple rim.	Munhata T641 (Ferembach et al. 1975: fig. 8:1) Megiddo (Loud 1948: pl. 19:31)
5	BT 1	Deposition 1	Bottle with thick flat base, wide globular body and flared simple rim.	

consistent with the general tradition of painted MB IIA pottery.

The jugs from the site and may be divided into the following categories:

Type JG1: Jug with Oval Body and Flat Base

TYPE JG1A: *everted rim* (fig. 5.15:1–2). Both examples of this form have a flat base and painted decoration. Fig. 5.15:1 has parallels with a jug from Kabri (Kempinski et al. 2002: fig. 5.58:5), although the latter is undecorated. Fig. 5.15:2 has a shorter ovoid body, long neck and a wide trefoil mouth; although the decoration is consistent within the repertoire of MB IIA painted vessels, there is no close parallel for this jug.

TYPE JG1B: *triangular rim* (fig. 5.15:3–4). Fig. 5.15:3 has a flat base and a rim with a pronounced exterior triangular profile. A jug with a similar rim, although more upright in stance, comes from Phase 4 at Tell el-Hayyat (Falconer and Magness-Gardiner 1984: fig. 16:7). The triangular profile on fig. 5.15:4 is smaller and the rim less everted, with painted decoration on the body and handle (fig.

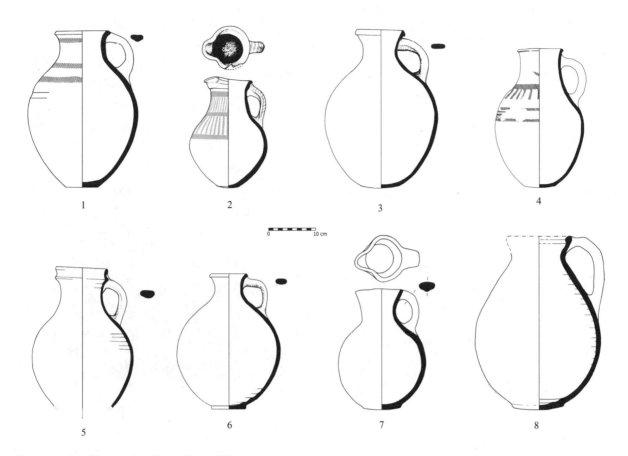

FIG. 5.15 *Jugs from Gesher, Types JG1 and JG2.*

No.	Type	GR/BR #	Description	Parallels
1	JG1A	Grave 14	Jug with oval body, flat base and everted rim. Painted decoration on upper body and neck.	
2	JG1A	Surface	Jug with oval body, flat base, trefoil mouth, and everted rim. Painted decoration on body, neck, and handle.	
3	JG1B	Grave 4B	Jug with oval body, flat base, and triangular rim.	Tell el-Hayyat 4 (Falconer and Magness-Gardiner 1984: fig. 16:7)
4	JG1B	Grave 18	Jug with oval body, slightly convex base, triangular rim. Painted decoration on body and handle.	Kabri T1050 (Kempinski et al. 2002: fig. 5.22.13), juglet with identical design; Kabri T990 (Kempinski et al. 2002: fig. 5.58.5), no decoration.
5	JG1C	Surface	Jug with upright ridged rim.	Jericho Tomb K3 (Kenyon 1965: fig. 93:4)
6	JG2A	Grave 10	Jug with rounded body, disc base, and simple rim.	
7	JG2A	Grave 16	Jug with rounded, globular body, disc base, trefoil mouth, and simple rim.	
8	JG2B	Surface	Red-slipped small jug with rounded body, convex, disc base, inward triangular rim.	

5.16). The same painted decoration appears on a jug from T3168 at Megiddo (Loud 1948: pl. 11:20), and two juglets from Tomb 1050 at Kabri (Kempinski et al. 2002: fig. 5.22:13–14). Close parallels may also be seen with a third piece from Kabri (Kempinski et al. 2002: fig. 5.58:5), although this piece is undecorated.

TYPE JG1C: *upright ridged rim* (Fig. 5.15:5).[6] The rim on this form has some similarities to a jug from Jericho (Kenyon 1965: fig. 93:14), although the body shapes are very different. As the piece is incomplete, the shape of the base is unknown; the body shape, however, is consistent with the Type JG1 category.

Type JG2: Jug with Rounded Body and Disc Base

TYPE JG2A: *simple rim* (fig. 5.15:6–7). Both examples from Gesher have wide rounded bodies; the disc base is more pronounced on fig 5.15:6. On both jugs the simple rim flares slightly outward; the wide neck and trefoil mouth on fig. 5.15:7 are consistent with the earlier phases of trefoil jugs and juglets in MB IIA (fig. 5.17).

TYPE JG2B: *inward triangular rim* (fig. 5.15:8). The rounded body and wide neck are typical of the Gesher repertoire of juglets, jugs and jars, although the red slip over the entire piece is rare at Gesher.[7] The disc base on this piece is slightly rounded. The wide neck has a concave groove running along the inside below the inward triangular rim.

5.2.5   Jars (SJ)

The jars from Gesher include both large and small handleless forms and larger two-handled store-jars. Most of the vessels have a rounded body and flat base, although some have a disc base. Both basic types appear with and without surface treatment and/or decoration.

While generally consistent with other MB IIA assemblages, the jars from Gesher differ in shape, size, and proportions from those found at coastal sites (Beck 2000b: 180; Beck 2000c: 247; Garfinkel and Bonfil 1990), as do the juglets and jugs discussed above. This most probably should be taken as reflective of regional differences and different

FIG. 5.16 *Painted jug (fig. 5.15:4).*

FIG. 5.17 *Jug with trefoil mouth (fig. 5.15:7).*

developmental patterns in the Jordan Valley region. Other characteristics, such as the painted decoration, also point to northern influences and an early MB IIA date.

The jars from Gesher have been divided into the following categories:

Type SJ1: Handleless Jar with Flat Base

Approximately one third of the jars found at Gesher are Type SJ1 store-jars (fig. 5.18). Handleless jars are common in the early phases of MB IIA and do not appear to continue past the middle of the period (Beck 2000b: 179, 320, fig. 10:31; Yogev 1985: 99). It has been suggested that this type of jar reflects influences from inland Syria (Amiran 1970: 166–67; Beck 2000b: 179). Within the category, there is considerable variation in rim shape and stance, and the jars have been further subdivided as follows:

Type SJ1A: *externally thickened rim* (5.18:1–3). The jars in this category have upright, externally thickened rims. The original publication of the Gesher material from 1986–1987 (Garfinkel and Bonfil 1990: fig. 1:4), cites a parallel for their fig. 1:4 with a jar from Tomb 2 at Rehov (Yogev 1985: fig. 3:2). Fig. 5.18:3 has a particularly pronounced exterior triangular section (fig. 5.19); a jar with a similar triangular profile was found in Dolmen 14 in the Golan (Epstein 1985: fig. 4:16).

Type SJ1B1: *flared flat rim* (fig. 5.18:4). This jar is characterized by a short neck and a strongly flared rim, flattened on the top. A similar jar from Tomb 8 at Rehov (Yogev 1985: fig. 3:1) has a ridged neck.

Type SJ1B2: *flared rim* (fig. 5.18:5–6). Two jars of this type were found at Gesher. There are no close parallels for this particular flared rim on small handleless jars (figs. 5.18:5; 5.20).

Type SJ1C: *externally molded rim* (fig. 5.18:7). The one example of this type at Gesher has two sets of incised bands around the upper body. A similar jar from Golan Dolmen 14 (Epstein 1985: fig. 4:18) is larger and without decoration.

Type SJ1D: *internal concave rim* (fig. 5.18:8).[8] The complete shape of the one jar of this type from Gesher is unknown, as its base is missing. Jars with similar concave rims and flat bases have been found at Aphek (Ory 1938: nos. 73–74).

Type SJ1D: *other/rim unknown* (fig. 5.18:9). The overall shape of this form is unknown, as it is broken below the neck. The painted decoration on the upper body and neck is consistent with the decoration on other pieces from the corpus.

Type SJ2: Small Handleless Jar

As noted above, one of these jars (fig. 5.21:1) has been previously published as a bottle (Garfinkel and Bonfil 1990: fig. 3:10); the general shape of these three forms, however, and their proportions are more consistent with small jars (Beck 2000b) than with bottles found at other sites, which either have much taller and narrower necks or rounded and squatter bodies (see discussion above). Within this category of small handleless jar, two types have been identified at Gesher.

Type SJ2A: *exterior triangular rim* (fig. 5.21:1–2). Both of these jars have a short wide neck, and a rim with an external triangular profile; fig. 5.21:1 has a rounded body. The base on fig. 5.21:2 is smaller and has a slight omphalos; the triangular profile is more pronounced on this piece as well. Parallels for these small jars have been found in Tomb 58 at Gibeon (Pritchard 1963: fig. 64:9–10) and Tomb 1513 at Lachish (Tufnell 1958: pl. 78:804).

Type SJ2B: *double ridged rim* (fig. 5.21:3). The one example of this type has a slightly convex disc base, round body with a wide neck and a slightly everted double ridged rim. The painted decoration consists of one black and one red painted band at mid-body and one red painted band at the base of the neck. A small jar with a similar rim was excavated at Hagosherim (Covello-Paran 1996: fig. 4:12). A larger handleless jar from Sidon with a disc base has a similar rim with more pronounced ridges (Doumet-Serhal 2001: pl. 7).

Type SJ3: Jar with Handles and Flat Base

The larger two-handled store-jars found at Gesher (fig. 5.22) are typical of those found elsewhere in MB IIA, although the proportions vary, as discussed below.

Type SJ3A: *thickened rim* (fig. 5.22:1–2). Both store-jars from this type have short necks and everted

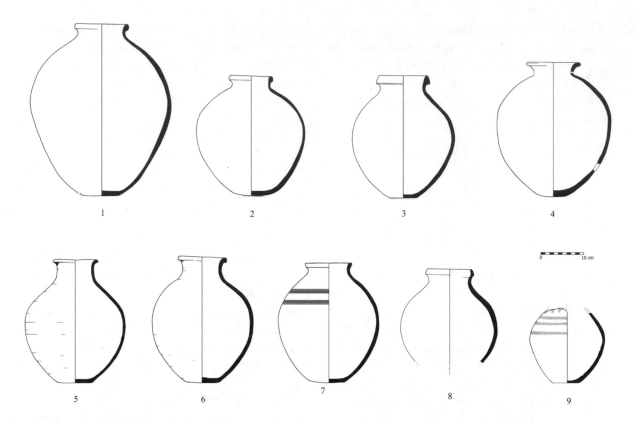

FIG. 5.18 *Jars from Gesher, Type SJ1.*

No.	TYPE	GR/BR #	DESCRIPTION	PARALLELS
1	SJ1A1	Grave 2	Handleless store-jar with flat base and externally thickened rim.	Rehov T2 (Yogev 1985: fig. 3:2)
2	SJ1A1	Grave 5	Handleless store-jar with flat base and externally thickened rim.	
3	SJ1A1	Grave 16	Handless store-jar with flat base and rim with external triangular profile.	Golan Dolmen 14 (Epstein 1985: fig. 4:16)
4	SJ1B1	Grave 7	Handleless store-jar with flat base and flared flat rim.	Rehov T8 (Yogev 1985: fig. 3:1); ridge around neck.
5	SJ1B2	Grave 23	Handleless store-jar with flat base and flared flat rim.	
6	SJ1B2	Grave 20	Handleless store-jar with flat base and everted thickened rim.	
7	SJ1C	Grave 1	Handleless store-jar with flat base and externally molded rim. Horizontal incised decoration on upper body.	Golan Dolmen 14 (Epstein 1985: fig. 4.18) Tell el-Hayyat 5 (Falconer and Magness-Gardiner 1984: fig. 13:8).
8	SJ1D	Surface	Handleless store-jar with internal concave rim.	Megiddo T3143 (Loud 1948: pl. 12:16) Aphek Grave 2 (Ory 1938: nos. 73, 74).
9	SJ1E	Grave 10	Handleless store-jar with flat base; rim unknown. Painted decoration on upper body.	

FIG. 5.19 *Handleless Jar, Type SJ1A (fig. 5.18:3).*

FIG. 5.20 *Handleless Jar, Type SJ1B2 (fig. 5.18:6).*

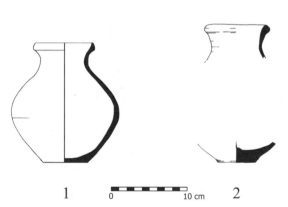

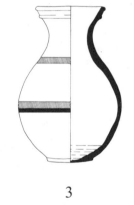

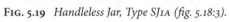

1   0   10 cm   2   3

FIG. 5.21 *Jars from Gesher, Type SJ2.*

No.	Type	GR/BR #	Description	Parallels
1	SJ2A	Grave 9	Small handleless jar with wide flat base, rounded body, short wide neck and exterior triangular rim.	Gibeon T58 (Pritchard 1963: fig. 64:9–10) Lachish T1513 (Tufnell 1958: pl. 78:804)
2	SJ2A	Deposition 4	Small handleless jar with wide flat base, rounded body, short wide neck and exterior triangular rim.	Gibeon T58 (Pritchard 1963: fig. 64:9–10) Lachish T1513 (Tufnell 1958: pl. 78:804)
3	SJ2B	Grave 17/ erosion	Small handleless jar with convex disc base, round body, wide neck and slightly everted double ridged rim. Painted decoration at mid-body and base of neck.	Hagosherim Tomb A (Covello-Paran 1996: fig. 4:12)

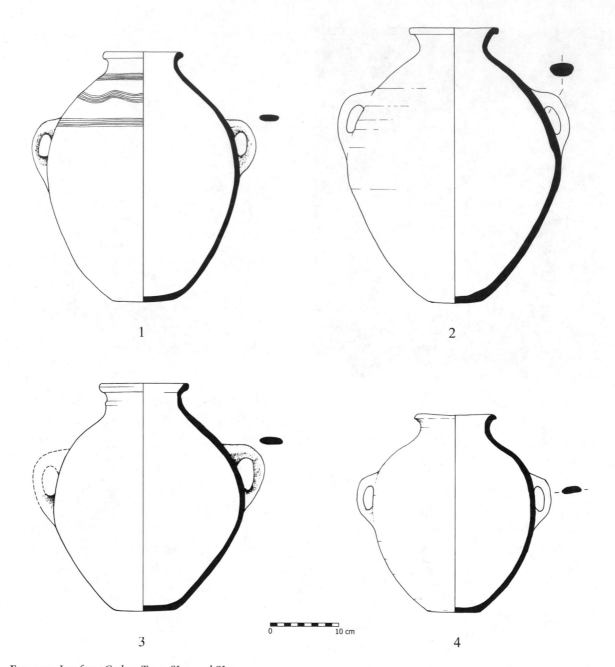

FIG. 5.22 *Jars from Gesher, Types SJ3A and SJ3B.*

No.	Type	GR/BR #	Description	Parallels
1	SJ3A	Grave 8	Jar with handles, flat base and thickened rim. Incised decoaration on upper body above handles.	Tell el-Hayyat 5 (Falconer and Magness-Gardiner 1984: fig. 13:14)
2	SJ3A	Grave 19	Jar with handles above mid-body, flat base and flat thickened rim.	
3	SJ3B	Grave 4b	Jar with handles, flat base and everted rim.	Tell el-Hayyat 5 (Falconer and Magness-Gardiner 1984: fig. 13:9)
4	SJ3B	Grave 21	Jar with handles, flat base and everted rim.	Tell el-Hayyat 5 (Falconer and Magness-Gardiner 1984: fig. 13:16).

FIG. 5.23 *Store-jar with incised decoration (fig. 5.22:1).*

FIG. 5.24 *Store-jar, Type SJ3A (fig. 5.22:2).*

thickened rims. Fig. 5.22:1, however, has a wider base and the handles are set at the widest point of the body; three bands of combed decoration run around the upper body and neck (fig. 5.23); Fig. 5.22:2 tapers to a smaller base and the handles are placed above the middle of the body (fig. 5.24).

TYPE SJ3B: *everted rim* (fig. 5.22:3–4). Both store-jars in this category have wide rounded bodies with the handles set just above the widest point (fig. 5.25). Jars with similar rims have been found in Phase 5 at Tell el-Hayyat (Falconer and Magness-Gardiner 1984: fig. 13:9, 16).

TYPE SJ3C1: *externally molded rim* (fig. 5.26:1–2). Store-jars with an externally molded rim are common in MB IIA; parallels exist with Phase 5 at Tell el-Hayyat (Falconer and Magness-Gardiner 1984: fig. 13:8).

TYPE SJ3C2: *externally molded square rim* (figs. 5.26:3–4; 5.27). The two store-jars of this type are wider and more rounded than the rest of the jar corpus at Gesher, with the handles set at the widest point of the body. Both also have deliberate openings cut into the side of the jars (fig. 5.27); the purpose for this is not clear, and there are no immediate parallels for this at other sites.

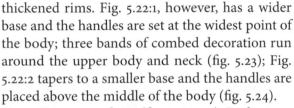

FIG. 5.25 *Store-jar, Type SJ3B (fig. 5.22:4).*

Type SJ4: Handleless Jar with Disc Base

This jar (fig. 5.28:1) differs from the rest of the Gesher corpus in both its disc base and its delicate profile. The outward triangular rim is also

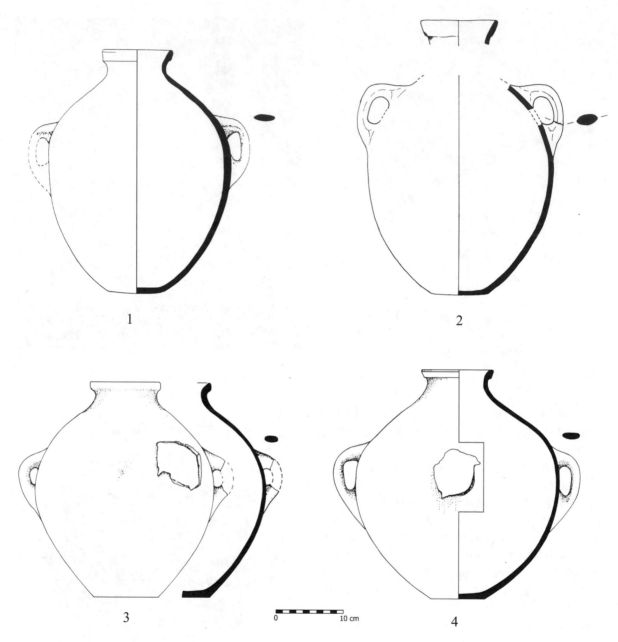

FIG. 5.26 *Jars from Gesher, Type SJ3C1.*

No.	Type	GR/BR #	Description	Parallels
1	SJ3C1	Grave 8	Jar with handles, flat base and externally molded rim.	Tell el-Hayyat 5 (Falconer and Magness-Gardiner 1984: fig. 13:8.
2	SJ3C1	Grave 18	Jar with handles, flat base and externally molded rim.	
3	SJ3C2	Grave 11	Jar with handles, flat base and everted rim. Deliberate opening cut in side of jar.	Tell el-Hayyat 5 (Falconer and Magness-Gardiner 1984: fig. 13:8)
4	SJ3C2	Grave 12	Jar with handles, flat base and externally molded rim. Deliberate opening cut in side of jar.	Tell el-Hayyat 5 (Falconer and Magness-Gardiner 1984: fig. 13:8)

FIG. 5.27 *Store-jars (Type SJ3C2) with deliberate openings cut in the side (figs. 5.26:3–4) .*

more everted than the more upright stance on the other handleless jars at Gesher. A similar jar from Aphek (Beck 1985: fig. 2:16) has a more pronounced profile.

Type SJ5: Jar with concave Base and Rim

This jar (figs. 5.28:2; 5.29), with a thin concave base – almost a low ring base – and a concave rim with an exterior profile, is unique in the Gesher corpus. The upper body and neck of the jar have red painted decoration in a geometric pattern, consisting of triangles, bands, and crossed lines, on the shoulders, neck and rim, consistent with Levantine Painted Ware; parts of a similar painted design of crossed lines can be seen on sherds from Phases 4 and 3 at Tell el-Hayyat (Falconer and Magness-Gardiner 1984: fig. 17). A jar from Phase B at Tel Ifshar has a similar, although more pronounced, concave rim and profile as well as painted decoration (Paley and Porath 1997: fig. 13.6:5).

5.3 SUMMARY

The ceramic corpus from the cemetery at Gesher is clearly consistent with the earliest phases of MB IIA. Yet, despite the inherent similarities with recognizable MB IIA forms, the Gesher materials also differ from other MB IIA corpora in several ways. In particular, the overall poor quality of the pottery is atypical for the period. As noted above, the Gesher ceramics are thick and heavy, often extremely lopsided, and made from coarse and poorly levigated clay. Frequently, the vessels are badly fired; there is often a large dark coarse core and the fabric deteriorates easily.

While the forms are clearly MB IIA, the typology of all of the Gesher ceramics is slightly different from similar forms attested in the coastal assemblages and from larger urban sites. In general, the bodies of all closed forms found at Gesher are wider and rounder than their basic typological counterpoint within the known MB IIA corpus. In

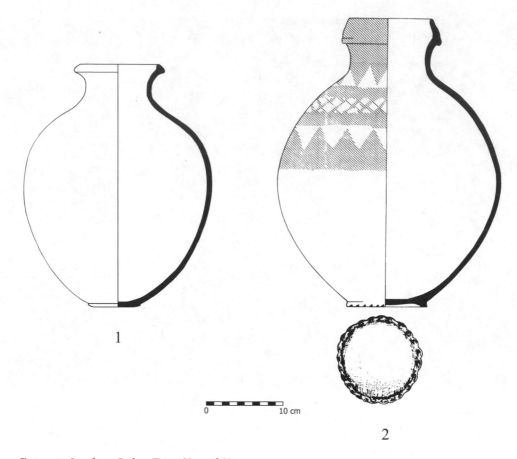

0   10 cm

FIG. 5.28 *Jars from Gesher, Types SJ4 and SJ5.*

No.	TYPE	GR/BR #	DESCRIPTION	PARALLELS
1	SJ4	Grave 10	Jar with disc base and outward triangular rim.	Aphek X19–X20 (Beck 1985: fig. 2:16)
2	SJ5	Grave 13	Jar with low ring base, concave rim. Painted decoration on upper body, neck, and rim.	Ifshar Phase B (Paley and Porath 1997: fig. 13.6:5), disc base.

FIG. 5.29 *Levantine Painted Ware Jar (fig. 5.28:2).*

particular, the jars with the maximum diameter in the center of the body are similar to those in the preceding EB IV/MB I (Beck 2000c: 247; Falconer and Magness-Gardiner 1984: 60–61). In addition to the difference in body shape, the necks of the closed forms are also shorter and wider than those attested elsewhere.

Syrian traditions may also have influenced the development of ceramics in the northern Jordan Valley. Several of the Gesher ceramics indicate a northern influence, such as the bottle (fig. 5.14:5) and the pieces with painted decoration, in par-

ticular those in the tradition of Levantine Painted Ware (see Tubb 1983, Gerstenblith 1983). These traditions are more visible in the material culture from the more peripheral areas of Canaan in MBIIA, which are those regions that would have been less strongly affected by the overall trend toward rapid urbanization. The differences notable in the Gesher ceramics help to highlight the different developmental patterns in early MB IIA in this region (Beck 2000c: 247; also see discussion in Maeir 1997a) and further illustrate the transitional nature of Gesher.

Notes

1   Some of these pieces, however, were too incomplete or lacking in diagnostics, and were not drawn and are not presented here in the accompanying illustrations.

2   The ceramics from the 1986–1987 excavations were originally published by tomb group (Garfinkel and Bonfil 1990). This material is presented again in this chapter, together with the ceramics found in 2002–2004; for the most part, the basic descriptions and categories established for the 1986–1987 corpus remain the same, but some changes have been made to the original order of presentation and typological descriptions in order to integrate the material with that found in the later excavations and to include information regarding MB IIA ceramics from more recent excavations.

3   See Chapter 6 for further discussion of this bowl in association with axes in mortuary contexts.

4   In the previous publication of the ceramics from the 1986–1987 excavations (Garfinkel and Bonfil 1990), S-shaped bowls were included in the general category of carinated bowls. Here, S-shaped bowls have been placed in a separate category.

5   In the first publication of ceramics from the cemetery, fig 5.21:1 was described by Garfinkel and Bonfil

as a bottle (1990: 136–37, fig. 3:10). In her comparative analysis of the material from Aphek, Beck (2000b: 178) placed this object within her category of small handleless jars (Type SJ3 at Aphek). As the general shape and the proportion of the rim diameter to the overall width of the body is consistent with this category as defined, and additional small jars of this type, which are typologically different from the bottle BT1, were found during the 2002–2004 excavations, fig. 5.21:1 has been moved to the category of small jars.

6   It should be noted that the authors disagree with some of the parallels cited for this form in its original publication (Hess 1990, and reproduced in this volume as Chapter 2); therefore they have not been cited in this chapter.

7   It should be noted that this piece was found in a heavily eroded area on the very edge of the road cut and not in any burial context; the only other vessel with red slip (fig. 5.14:4) was also a surface find.

8   Again, it should be noted that the authors disagree with some of the parallels cited for this form in its original publication (see above, n. 6); therefore, they have not been cited in this chapter.

Chapter 6

The Bronzes

by Yosef Garfinkel and Susan Cohen

6.1 INTRODUCTION

A total of thirteen bronze artifacts were found at Gesher (Tables 6.1–2). One item was found as part of the surface collection (see Chapter Two); the remaining twelve bronzes were excavated from eight separate burials (Graves 2, 5, 12–14, 18–19, and 22). This chapter discusses the comparative archaeological context of these objects, while details regarding the chemical composition and metallurgical analysis of the bronzes are presented in Chapter 7.

6.2 THE DUCKBILL AXES

Three duckbill axes have been excavated at Gesher from Graves 2, 12, and 13 (fig. 6.1). The axe from Grave 2 (Item 23) was decorated with two incised lines (figs. 6.2–3). Similar decoration is attested on one of the two duckbill axes from Safed (Damati and Stepanski 1996: fig. 10:1) and on an axe from Esh-Shejara (Gerstenblith 1983: fig. 36:3). The two axes from Graves 12 and 13 (Items 46 and 48) are undecorated (figs. 6.4–5), and have numerous parallels within the Middle Bronze Age Canaanite repertoire (Table 6.3).[1]

The duckbill axe first appears as early as the 20th century BCE and is one of the typological markers of the beginning of the Middle Bronze Age in Canaan. Duckbill axes have been found throughout the Near East, including Mesopotamia, Anatolia, Cyprus, and Egypt (Garfinkel 2001). In Canaan specifically, duckbill axes have been found at Beth Shan (Oren 1971; 1973), Kabri (Kempinski et al. 2002), Rehov (Yogev 1985), and Safed (Damati and Stepanski 1996).[2]

Nails (Items 23a and 47) were found in association with two of the axes at Gesher, from Graves 2 and 12 (figs. 6.6–7); in the case of the axe from Grave 2, the nail was still attached (fig. 6.3).[3] From these finds it is possible to comment on the methods of hafting in relation to the axes. Evidence suggests that the handle of the axe was fixed to the socket using nails hammered in at the top of the socket (Shalev 2002: 310). Similar hafting is also attested on socket axes from Kitan, Ginosar, and Sukas (Miron 1992: pls. 16:262, 17:270; Epstein 1974: fig. 12:2; Thrane 1978: fig. 85:86). Furthermore, fragments of wood recovered from a duckbill axe found in Tomb 990 at Kabri (Scheftelowitz and Gershuny 2002: 30) also support this suggestion.

TABLE 6.1 The bronze items from Gesher.

GRAVE	DUCKBILL AXE	SOCKET AXE	NAIL	SPEARHEAD	TOGGLE PIN	TOTAL
Topsoil				1		1
G-2	1		1	1		3
G-5					1	1
G-12	1		1			2
G-13	1			1		2
G-14		1				1
G-18				1		1
G-19				1		1
G-22				1		1
Total	3	1	2	6	1	**13**

TABLE 6.2 Bronze items from Gesher listed by size and weight.

ITEM #	GRAVE	TYPE	WEIGHT (IN GR)	LENGTH (IN MM)	WIDTH (IN MM)	THICKNESS (IN MM)	NOTES
48	G-13	Duckbill axe	220.8	102	46	24	
46	G-12	Duckbill axe	218.4	101	55	23	
23	G-2	Duckbill axe	190.7	103	43	22	decorated
45	G-14	Socket axe	158.8	129	18	14	
12	G-5	Toggle pin	48.3	238	17/10		decorated
42	G-13	Spearhead	47.6	190	35	14	Twine on socket OxA 1955 3640±70 bp
16	G-2	Spearhead	44.6	131	31	10	
49	topsoil	Spearhead	33.5	125	26	12	
16	G-18	Spearhead	22.2	132	20	12	Twine on socket
21	G-19	Spearhead	17.4	112	16	10	
27	G-22	Spearhead	26.7	135	24	10	Wood fragment in socket
23a	G-2	Nail	1.0	23	6	3	Fixed to axe (Item 23)
47	G-12	Nail	0.4	14+	3	3	Near axe (Item 46)

It is also probable that the axe handles were bent, rather than straight. For example, in the iconographic evidence at Beni Hasan showing foreigners carrying duckbill axes (Newberry 1893), the handles of the axes are bent. Further, bent axe handles have been found at Baghouz (du Mesnil du Buisson 1948), and a partially preserved wooden axe handle was also found in a Middle Bronze Age burial in the recent excavations at Sidon (Doumet-Serhal 2002: 189).[4]

6.3   THE SOCKET AXE

The socket axe at Gesher (fig. 6.8) was found in Grave 14 inside a shallow bowl with four knobs. This combination of axe and knobbed shallow bowl has been reported from other Middle Bronze cemeteries, as in Grave 990 at Kabri (Scheftelowitz and Gershuny 2002: 30),[5] Tomb 1 in Ginosar (Epstein 1974: fig. 7:15), and at Tel Sukas (Thrane 1978). These graves, however, contain a number of individu-

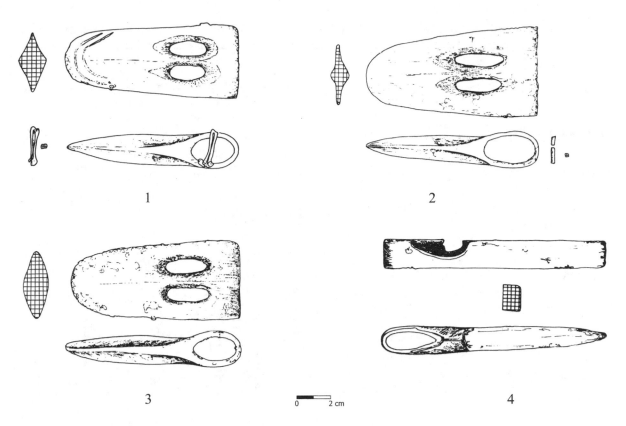

1

2

3

4

0 2 cm

FIG. 6.1 *Drawings of duckbill axes and socketed axe found at Gesher.*

FIG. 6.2 *Duckbill axe with decoration and nail from Grave 2, top view.*

FIG. 6.3
Duckbill axe with decoration and nail from Grave 2, side view.

FIG. 6.4
Duckbill axe from Grave 12.

FIG. 6.5
Duckbill axe from Grave 13.

TABLE 6.3 Duckbill axes found at MB IIA sites in Canaan.

SITE NAME	QUANTITY	CONTEXT	REFERENCE
'Ein Sa'ed	1	–	Epstein and Guttman 1972: 290
Shamir	1	Surface	Miron 1992: 54
Tel Dan	1	Glacis	Biran 1994: 63–65; Ilan 1992
Safed	2	–	Miron 1992: 54 (Bahat excavations)
Safed	2	Tomb	Damati and Stepanski 1996: fig. 10
Meron	1	Tomb 1	Tpilinsky 1962: 25; Miron 1992: 53
esh-Shejara	1	–	Gerstenblith 1983: fig. 36:3
Kabri	1	Tomb 990	Scheftelowitz and Gershuny 2002
Nahariya	1	–	Miron 1992: 53
Tell Kurdaneh	1	Tomb	Maisler 1939: 154; Miron 1992: 54
Beth Shean	1	Tomb 92	Oren 1971; 1973: 61–67
Tel Rehov	1	Tomb 2	Yogev 1985: 104–5
'Ein es-Samiyeh	2	Cemetery	Dever 1975: 30; Miron 1992 (from the market)
Aphek	2	Two tombs	Miron 1992: 54
Ashkelon	1	–	Maxwell-Hyslop 1949: 121

FIG. 6.6 *Close-up of nail from duckbill axe in Grave 2.*

FIG. 6.7 *Nail associated with duckbill axe from Grave 2.*

FIG. 6.8 *Socket axe from Grave 14.*

als buried over a period of time and, therefore, no direct connection can be made between the axe and the knobbed bowl. Socket axes have also been uncovered at other Canaanite sites, such as Megiddo, Hazor, and Jericho.

The socket axe is a later form than the duckbill axe. The Gesher example is consistent with Miron's Type I (1992), the earliest of the three categories, and the Gesher socket axe may be one of the earliest examples of this type uncovered to date. The presence of a socket axe in addition to the duckbill axes at Gesher may indicate that the cemetery was

in use for a longer span of time than previously anticipated; this suggestion is also supported by some of the ceramic evidence, as noted in Chapter 5.

6.4   The Spearheads

Seven spearheads have been found at Gesher (fig. 6.9), one from the surface collection (Hess 1990; see Chapter 2) and six from burial contexts in Graves 2, 13, 18–19, and 22 (figs. 6.10–14).[6] The socketed spearhead is generally considered to be a characteristic weapon of MB IIA (Dever 1975: 23;

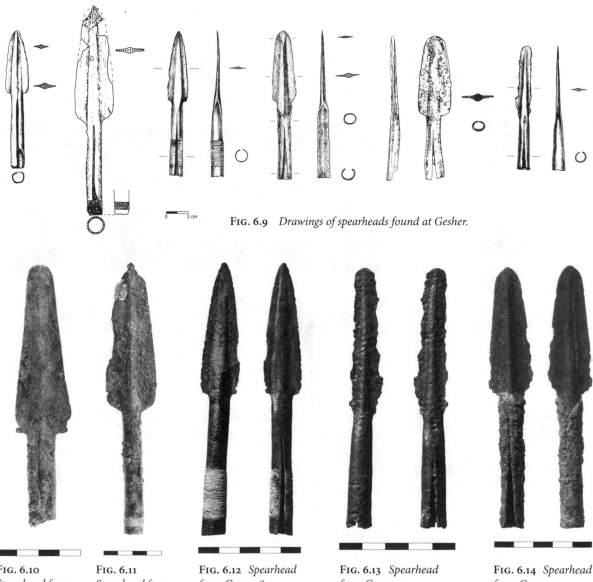

Fig. 6.9 *Drawings of spearheads found at Gesher.*

Fig. 6.10
Spearhead from Grave 2.

Fig. 6.11
Spearhead from Grave 13.

Fig. 6.12 *Spearhead from Grave 18.*

Fig. 6.13 *Spearhead from Grave 19.*

Fig. 6.14 *Spearhead from Grave 22.*

TABLE 6.4 Socketed spearheads found at MB IIA sites in Canaan.

SITE NAME	QUANTITY	CONTEXT	REFERENCE
Ain es-Samiyeh	2	unknown	Dever 1975 figs. 1:2–3
Ajjul	2	Tomb 1417	Tufnell 1962: fig. 10:18; Petrie 1932: pl. XIV:75
Aphek	2	Graves 2 and 4	Ory 1938: pl. 32 B:5 and 32 B:7
Barqai	3	Burial, 2nd phase	Gophna and Sussman 1969: fig. 4:13–15; pl. 2:2–3
Beth Shan	1	Tomb 92	Oren 1971: fig. 2:2, tbl. 8:2; Oren 1973: fig. 24:13
Gibeon	2	Tomb 58	Pritchard 1963: figs. 64:12 and 64:13
Ginosar	3	Tombs 1, 2/3 and 4	Epstein 1974: figs. 7:14, 11:23, 18:1.
Kfar Szold	1	Tomb	Epstein 1974: fig 4:10; pl. 3:10.
Megiddo	8	Tombs 911A1, 911C, 911D, 912B, 912D	Guy 1938 figs. 170:3–4; pls. 118:6–8, 120:13, 122:5–7, 125:12, 133:7
Rehov	2	Tomb 2	Yogev 1985: figs. 4:4–5; pls. 18:10–11.
Safed	12	Burial cave	Damati and Stepansky 1996: figs. 12–13.

FIG. 6.15 *Close-up of twine binding on spearhead from Grave 13.*

FIG. 6.16 *Close-up of twine binding on spearhead from Grave 18.*

Gerstenblith 1983: 91; Oren 1971; Tubb 1985: 189). Philip's (1989) detailed work on metal weapons from the Levant divides spearheads into a number of different categories, of which Types 7 and 8 provide the closest parallels for the spearheads from Gesher. In Canaan, socketed spearheads have been found in mortuary contexts at Rehov (Yogev 1985), Barqai (Gophna and Sussman 1969), Beth Shean (Oren 1971), Ginosar (Epstein 1974), Megiddo (Guy 1938), Aphek (Ory 1938), and Kfar Szold (Epstein 1974; Table 6.4).

In many cases for the socketed spearhead, rather than using a nail as was the case for the axes, a twine binding would have been used to secure the end of the socket and the joint between the edges of the socket and the shaft (Philip 1989: 88). This method is clearly illustrated by the twine still extant on the spearheads from Graves 13 and 18 (Items 43 and 66; figs. 6.15–16; see also Chapter 8). Additional examples of twine bindings were found at Megiddo (Guy 1938: fig. 170:5, pl. 149:4) and Ginosar (Epstein 1974: fig. 13:23).

FIG. 6.17 *Toggle pin.*

FIG. 6.18 *Close-up of the "eye" of the toggle pin.*

FIG. 6.19 *Close-up of the herringbone pattern on the toggle pin.*

6.5 THE TOGGLE PIN

One toggle pin, 23.8 cm long, was found at Gesher in Grave 5 (Item 12; fig. 6.17). The pin was oriented with the head pointing toward the legs of the individual (see fig. 3.29). This orientation of the toggle pin is also attested at Dhahrat el-Humraiya (Ory 1948: 77), Graves 1, 4, and 12 at Tell Sukas (Thrane 1978) and Grave 6 at Rehov (Yogev 1985).

The head of the pin has a mushroom shape; a square eye is located near the center of the pin (fig. 6.18), and the base is pointed. The upper part of the body is decorated with a delicate incised herringbone pattern that encircles the body of the pin (fig. 6.19). Other examples of elongated toggle pins with herringbone incisions on the upper half of the pin are attested at other Middle Bronze Age sites such as Safed (Damati and Stepanski 1996: fig. 18:7), Hagosherim (Covello-Paran 1996: fig. 5:1), Nahariya (Dothan 1956: pl. 4/D:2), and Byblos (Tufnell and Ward 1996: figs. 10:251, 254–55, 261, 266; see fig 6.20). Other pins have been found at Jericho (Kenyon 1960), Safed (Damati and Stepanski 1996), and Rehov (Yogev 1985).

Toggle pins are part of the clothing typical of the Middle and Late Bronze Ages in the Levant. The presence of toggle pins in burials indicates that the dead were buried with clothing, as indicated by the finds at Jericho (Kenyon 1960: 266). Iconography from Mari (Parrot 1962: pl. XI: 2–4, pl. XII: 3) shows people with a toggle pin on the breast, with the head of the pin facing down (fig. 6.21).

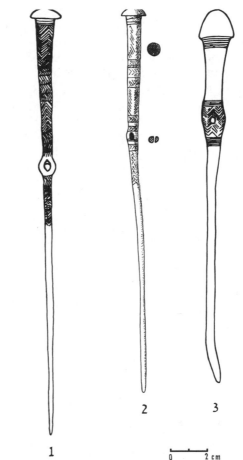

1   2   3

0   2 cm

FIG. 6.20 *Toggle pins from early MB IIA sites with incised herringbone decoration. Gesher, Zefat (Damati and Stepanski 1996: fig. 18:7), and Byblos (Garfinkel and Bonfil 1990: fig. 6).*

FIG. 6.21 *Middle Bronze engravings from Mari show three figures wearing toggle pins. Note that the pin is affixed with its head towards the ground and the tip pointing upwards (Parrot 1962: pls. XI:2–4, XII:3).*

NOTES

1 The most comprehensive recent survey of axes and their typology is that complied by Miron (1992). It should be noted, however, that Miron combined eye-axes and duckbill axes into one category; his catalogue also included those of unknown provenience in museums and private collections.

2 It is interesting to note that no duckbill axes are attested at cities such as Megiddo, Hazor, and Jericho, perhaps because these cities were established at a later stage of the Middle Bronze Age, by which time this axe form was no longer in use.

3 This situation is also attested in a find from Ugarit (Schaeffer 1962: 224, fig. 26:6).

4 The excavators do not specify whether this was a duckbill or a socket axe.

5 Note, however, that the axe found at Kabri is a duckbill axe rather than a socket axe, and the bowl in which it was found is described as having three bar handles (Scheftelowitz and Gershuny 2002: 30), whereas the bowl found at Gesher has four small knob handles.

6 The three spearheads from the 2002–2004 excavations have also been published separately (Cohen 2005).

Chapter 7

Metallurgical Analysis

by Sariel Shalev

7.1 INTRODUCTION

This chapter presents the metallurgical analysis of the bronze artifacts excavated from the Gesher cemetery.[1] The goal of this study is to examine the chemical composition of the metal objects and the technological processes involved in producing them. These results are then compared typologically to other weapons from Middle Bronze Age contexts in order to better understand their archaeological context.

7.2 METHODOLOGY

This section only applies to the eight objects recovered from the 1986–1987 excavations; the data pertaining to the analysis of the objects from the 2002–2004 excavations is presented in Table 7.5. Samples were taken from the objects for the purpose of metallurgical and metallographic analyses. Minute chips of less than a centimeter in size were removed by hand with the aid of a jeweler's saw or a small drill with a 0.7 mm diameter bit. The mode of sampling was chosen according to size and preservation condition of the finds in order to minimize the visible damage to the artifact.

The samples were hot mounted in acrylic mixed with copper powder, ground and polished to 1 micron. The surface of the polished sample was then etched for metallographic examination with ammonical hydrogen peroxide or ferric chloride and hydrochloric acid diluted in water or ethanol. An optical metallographic microscope with magnification of up to 1000× was employed in order to examine the microstructure of the metal preserving the cast properties as well as any further thermal and mechanical treatment of the object. Hardness testing of the material was conducted, when possible, using a Vickers diamond pyramid shaped tester. The samples were then re-polished for electron probe microanalysis.

Analyses were made using the CAMEBAX electron probe micro-analyzer (EPMA) in the Department of Materials, Oxford University. The analyses were made over three 50 micron squares on each sample. The accelerating voltage was 25kEV, the beam current 100nA and the counting time per element 10 seconds. The elements analyzed, X-ray lines used, and detection limits are specified in Table 7.1.

TABLE 7.1   Technical specifications for CAMEBAX EPMA.

ELEMENT	ENERGY-LINE	LIMIT OF DETECTION
Iron (*Fe*)	Kα	0.01 W%
Cobalt (*Co*)	Kα	0.01 W%
Nickel (*Ni*)	Kα	0.01 W%
Copper (*Cu*)	Kα	0.01 W%
Zinc (*Zn*)	Kα	0.02 W%
Arsenic (*As*)	Lα	0.02 W%
Silver (*Ag*)	Lα	0.02 W%
Tin (*Sn*)	Lα	0.01 W%
Antimony (*Sbn*)	Lα	0.02 W%
Gold (*Au*)	Mα	0.04 W%
Lead (*Pb*)	Mα	0.03 W%
Bismuth (*Bi*)	Mα	0.01 W%

TABLE 7.2   Typological specifications of the metal objects.

No.	OBJECT	REG. NO.	WEIGHT (g)	LENGTH (cm)	WIDTH (cm)	THICK. (cm)	DIAM. (cm)	SAMPLING AREA
1	Duckbill Axe	89-556	191.0	10.3	4.3	2.2	2.7	Side of blade
2	Duckbill Axe	89-590	221.0	10.2	4.6	2.4	2.2	Side of blade
3	Duckbill Axe	89-588	218.0	10.1	5.5	2.3	2.6	Near the socket
4	Socket Axe	89-587	159.0	12.9	1.8	1.4	2.6	Drilling inside socket
5	Spearhead	89-559	44.0	13.1	3.1	1.0	1.5	Near the socket
6	Spearhead	89-584	46.0	19.0	3.5	1.4	1.0	Break in blade
7	Spearhead	89-591	34.0	12.5	2.6	1.2	1.2	Break in blade
8	Toggle Pin	89-555	48.0	23.8		1.0	1.7	Drilling, head of pin
9	Spearhead	1103	22.2	13.2	2.0	1.2	1.2	Near the socket
10	Spearhead	1163	17.4	11.2	1.6	1.0	1.0	Near the socket
11	Spearhead	1193	26.7	13.5	2.4	1.0	1.1	Near the socket

TABLE 7.3   Chemical composition (%Wt) of the metal objects.

No.	CU	AS	SN	FE	CO	NI	ZN	AG	SB	AU	PB	BI
1	66.45	0.20	15.82	0.18	n.d.	0.07	n.d.	0.03	0.01	n.d.	17.11	0.10
2	95.31	3.23	0.02	0.32	0.01	n.d.	n.d.	0.10	0.03	0.05	0.78	0.14
3	86.81	2.04	0.13	0.38	0.01	0.02	0.08	0.18	0.07	0.03	10.21	0.04
4	93.71	3.47	0.03	2.27	0.03	0.37	n.d.	0.03	0.03	n.d.	0.04	n.d.
5	96.46	1.62	n.d.	0.65	0.02	0.65	n.d.	0.12	0.02	n.d.	0.49	n.d.
6	96.98	0.68	0.01	0.32	0.01	0.75	0.03	0.12	0.01	n.d.	1.08	0.01
7	97.22	0.74	0.01	0.62	n.d.	0.11	n.d.	0.09	0.03	n.d.	1.17	n.d.
8	96.41	1.35	0.03	0.28	0.02	0.05	0.03	0.04	0.01	n.d.	1.75	0.01

7.3   RESULTS

The results are presented on the next pages in three different tables detailing the typological affinities of the finds (Table 7.2), their chemical composition (Table 7.3), and the metallographic analysis (Table 7.4).

7.4   DISCUSSION

7.4.1   *The Duckbill Axes*

The duckbill axes excavated at Gesher belong to a large typological group common in the north of Palestine. Apart from a few specimens found out of archaeological context, such axes have only been found in tombs dated to the Middle Bronze Age IIA. Using the context of the other burial gifts in the tombs in which they were found (Graves 2, 13, and 12, respectively), these axes are dated to the beginning of the MBIIA, the first half of the 20th century BCE (Garfinkel and Bonfil 1990: 143–44).

This axe type was manufactured by the following method. It was cast in a two-piece stone mold with a core, probably of clay, inserted for the production of the hollow socket. Three fragments of such stone molds were found in Byblos, two of which were found out of context (Dunand 1954: 96, pl. 184; 1939: 20, pl. 108) and one in Strata 1–10 (Dunand 1939: 198, pl. 108) of the Middle Bronze Age II. The mold was made from two flat steatite slabs, joined by means of at least two drilled holes. One of the connecting holes is situated at the center of the back part of the mold, while the other is on one of the front sides of the blade.

A wide conical sprue was left as a runner at the front of the carved blade for pouring in the molten metal. No risers are visible on the mold, so it can be assumed that the runner was wide enough to let the gases escape during casting. In such two-part stone molds, a direct casting of metal could have been performed or wax models could have been prepared for a later "lost wax" metal casting. After casting, the metal was removed. The conical block of metal now filling the sprue was broken off the front of the blade and was probably saved for re-melting.

The cast axe then underwent further thermal and mechanical treatment by being annealed and hammered, especially on the blade edge. This treatment is visible in the microstructure of the metal in Gesher samples (Table 7.4:1–2; compare to untreated areas in Table 7.4:3), as well as in other duckbill axes (Branigan et al. 1976: 18). This process

TABLE 7.4   Metallographic analysis of cut samples.

No	Sample	Hardness	Corrosion	Coring	Annealing	Hammering	Crystals size	Thic. Reduc.
1	Duckbill Axe - from blade	113Hv2.5	Inter granular + inclusions	Only in corrosion	~650*C Twinning	Slip traces	15-20µm	15-20%
2	Duckbill Axe - from blade	140Hv2.5	Inter dendritic + S inclusions	Mainly α preserved	<550*C	Little slip traces	10-15µm	
3	Duckbill Axe - from socket	(corroded)	Inter dendritic + S, Pb inclusions	Mainly α preserved	No visible	No visible slip traces	Left as-cast	No reduction from the cast
5	Socket Spear - from socket	(corroded)	Inter granular + S elong. inclus.	Fully homogenized	~650*C Twinning	No final cold work	40-60µm	
6	Socket Spear - from blade	(corroded)	Inter granular + S elong. inclus.	Fully homogenized	<600*C Twinning	Slip traces & deform crystals	25-30µm	~30%
7	Socket Spear - from blade	(corroded)	Inter granular + S, Pb elong. inc.	Fully homogenized	<600*C Twinning	Slip traces & deform crystals	15-25µm	~30%

was probably carried out in order to mainly sharpen and slightly harden the blade. The hammering process of the blade was not massive, considering the relatively low level of hardness (not exceeding 140Hv in the Gesher duckbills axes), when an alloy of copper with three percent arsenic or more than 13 percent tin could be hammered, as in the case of dagger blades (Shalev 1996: 13), to a hardness of more then 200Hv and 240Hv, respectively. (For details of the metal properties of such alloys see Northover 1989). The axe was secured to a wooden handle inserted into the socket by means of nails hammered into the handle immediately above the top of the axe (Kan-Cipor-Meron 2003: fig. 17; Philip 1995a: fig. 1). Two such nails were found attached by corrosion to the top of the socket of axe No. 1 from Gesher, and a single nail, probably used similarly, was found beside axe No. 3 (see discussion in Chapter 6).

All metallurgical analyses of duckbill axes carried out to date have indicated that tin bronze (5–15 percent Sn) with varying amount of lead (reaching up to 25 percent Pb) was used for their manufacture (Branigan et al. 1976: 17, 22–23; Birmingham 1977; Oren 1971: 111, 128–29; Yogev 1985: 90–109; Phillip 1991: 94; Miron 1992; Shalev 2000: 281; 2002: 307, 310–11). The chemical composition of axe No. 1 from Gesher fits in very well with this group. The level of corrosion, mainly in grains boundaries, may have slightly affected the original amount of tin that could be estimated to 14–15 percent in the original cast. This data matches the metallurgical analyses of other examples from Ein Samiyeh, Nahariya, Rehov, and Kabri, and points to the existence of an industry producing items of high, controlled metallurgical quality (Shalev 2002: 310).

The other two duckbill axes (Nos. 2–3 in Table 7.2) present a different industry producing similar objects from another kind of metal, copper alloyed with two to three percent arsenic instead of tin. This is the first time that duckbill axes are found to be made from this traditional local material known in the metal industry of the eastern Levant from the end of the third millennium BCE (Philip 1991: 93–104) and found to be relatively popular in the Middle Bronze Age production of weapons, tools,

and ornaments (i.e., objects 4–5, 8 from Gesher; see Table 7.2; Philip 1991; Shalev 2000). Determinations of the hardness of these arsenic copper items (Northover 1989) show that the use of arsenical alloy did not affect the quality of the object.

The presence of lead in appreciable quantities in some cases (17 percent Pb in axe No. 1, and 10 percent Pb in axe No. 3 from Gesher) is unique to this type of metal product, with no known parallels in any other Middle Bronze Age type of metal objects from Palestine (Shalev 2000: 281). Based on lab experiments (detailed in Shalev 2002: 311), it may be concluded that in the case of the production of duckbill axes from both known alloys, lead was intentionally added in significant quantities to improve the fluidity of the melt, which made the casting of these relatively thick objects better and easier while preserving the thermal and mechanical properties of the original alloys.

7.4.2 *The Socket Axe*

Like the duckbill axe, the socket axe belongs to a large typological group. The production method of this type is similar to the one described above in detail for the duckbill axe. Fragments of steatite two-piece molds for casting this type of axe were found in Megiddo, Byblos, and Tel el-Daba (Miron 1992). In several cases, as in the former type, metal nails for securing the wooden handle are still found on top of the socket (Philip 1995a: fig. 1).

As with the duckbill axes, all chemical analyses of this type known to date show a tin bronze metal composition of 5–14 percent tin with up to 9 percent lead (Guy 1938: 161; Birmingham 1977: 115; Philip 1991: 94; Rosenfeld et al. 1997: tbl. 1). In contrast, the socket axe from Gesher is made of arsenical copper (3.5 percent As) with a relatively high iron impurity of 2 percent Fe. This detected level of iron is higher than other known analyses of MBII axes but fits well with some arsenical coppers from the same period, including a similar axe from Fasuta (0.7 percent Fe), a belt buckle from Jericho (1.4 percent Fe; Khalil 1980), toggle pins from Rishon Le-Zion (2 and 4 percent Fe; Kan-Cipor-Meron 2003: tbl. 6: RL-15 and 18, and tbl. 10).

TABLE 7.5 ICP-AES analysis of the spearheads (%Wt). Nos. 9–11: Analysis conducted by I. Segal, the Geological Survey of Israel; Nos. 5–7: EPMA results are relisted from Table 7.3, for ease of comparison.

No.	Cu	As	Sn	Fe	Co	Ni	Zn	Ag	Sb	Au	Pb	Bi
9	92.5	1.50	0.01	0.75		0.0 2	0.12	0.03	0.01		1.30	
10	90.4	2.20	2.31	0.50		tr.	0.01	0.07	0.02		1.00	
11	60.8[2]	0.28	11.00	0.34		0.02	0.02	0.02	0.02		0.43	
5	96.46	1.62	n.d.	0.65	0.02	0.65	n.d.	0.12	0.02	n.d.	0.49	n.d.
6	96.98	0.68	0.01	0.32	0.01	0.75	0.03	0.12	0.01	n.d.	1.08	0.01
7	97.22	0.74	0.01	0.62	n.d.	0.11	n.d.	0.09	0.03	n.d.	1.17	n.d.

7.4.3 The Socketed Spearheads

The metallographic analyses of the spearheads from Gesher present a different mode of production than that used for the manufacturing of the axes. This process would appear to have been essentially similar to that described by Guy (1938: 164) and replicated in an experiment for the production of socketed points (Bucholz and Drescher 1987: 47, fig. 7). The final shape of all spearheads from Gesher was dictated by cycles of annealing and hammering as testified by the annealing twins, size of crystals and slip traces, as detailed in Table 7.4:5–7. After casting, they were homogenized by re-heating to a temperature that exceeded 600° C and then hammered and annealed. Final cold work visible in the metallography of the blade probably aimed at reaching a hard effective blade of a hardness higher than 115Hv. This left the socket in a much softer state without any signs of final hammering, probably for enabling a tight and easy connection to the wooden pole by means of thin twine. Twine remains are still extant on the socket of spearheads No. 6 (Garfinkel and Bonfil 1990: 140–41) and No. 9 (see discussion in Chapter 8).

The compositional results of metal analyses of the socketed spearheads from Gesher represent the whole variety of known MB IIA copper alloys. Spearheads Nos. 5–7 and 9 were made of arsenical copper with 0.7–1.6 percent As, no tin, and some lead (0.5–1.3 percent Pb). Traces of iron (0.5–0.8 percent Fe) and in some cases (Nos. 5–6) also nickel

(up to 0.8 percent Ni) are also typical to this group. No parallels to this composition are known from the scarce analyses of this type of spearhead elsewhere. Spearhead No. 10 was made of copper with the same quantities of arsenic (2.2 percent) and tin (2.3 percent). The rest is similar to the former group and includes 1 percent lead and 0.5 percent iron. Close compositions were found in the analysis of socketed spearheads from Rehov (Shenberg 1985: 112) and in one of the three spearhead analyses from Aphek (No. 20; Shalev 2000: 283). The analysis of spearhead No. 11 shows a corrosion product and therefore the relative quantities are not reliable. Nevertheless, it is reflecting what was probably in its original state a low tin bronze like object No. 21 from Aphek (2.2 percent Sn; Shalev 2000: 283). or medium tin bronze like the objects from Fasuta (6.7–7.7 percent Sn; Shalev 2000: 283), with only traces of arsenic and less than 0.5 percent lead.

7.4.4 The Toggle Pin

The toggle pin from Gesher is a rare example, in its huge size and delicate decoration (Garfinkel and Bonfil 1990: 134), of a well-known MB II type of which hundreds of simpler and different examples have been found (Gerstenblith 1983: 94–95; Henschel-Simon 1938). The specimen from Gesher was made of arsenical copper of 1.4 percent As and lead in the volume of 1.8 percent Pb. No tin was found and the iron impurity did not exceed 0.3 percent Fe. None of its typological parallels has yet been analyzed for comparison. The toggle pin's metal composition fits well with some of the socketed spearheads (Nos. 6–7, 9) from Gesher but does not have any good parallels in the analyses of simpler types of toggle pins from the same period in other sites such as Kabri (Shalev 2002: 311–15), Rishon Le-Zion (Kan-Cipor-Miron 2003: tbl. 6.10), and Jericho (Khalil 1980: 124–35).

NOTES

1　The metal objects were analyzed by the author with the help of J. P. Northover in the Department of Materials at Oxford University.

2　The analysis of 1193 also includes 0.02 Mn; The total of seventy-two percent metal in this sample shows a corrosion product. Therefore, the quantitative results are not representing the original metal composition.

Chapter 8

The Organic Materials

by Susan Cohen and Nili Liphschitz

8.1 THE TWINE FROM THE SPEARHEAD FROM GRAVE 18 (S. COHEN)

The twine found on the spearhead from Grave 18 starts 1.0 cm from the base of the socket and wraps around 2.4 cm of the socket (see figs. 6.12 and 6.16 in Chapter 6). In many cases of socketed spearheads commonly found in MB IIA contexts, a twine binding would have been used to secure the end of the socket and the joint between the edges of the socket and the shaft (Philip 1989: 88); this method is clearly illustrated by the twine still extant on the example from Gesher.

The examination of the twine was conducted by Azriel Gorski of the Science and Antiquities Group at the Hebrew University of Jerusalem. Analysis indicates that it is made of flax, rather than an animal product such as sinew. Two strands of flax were used in this instance, twisted together to form the twine that was then wrapped around the socket of the spearhead.

The two fibers were examined by transmitted light and polarized light microscopy (figs. 8.1–4). During the examination, a non-human white hair was found in association with one of the flax fibers (fig. 8.5). It was not possible to determine which

animal species this hair belonged to, or, in fact, whether this hair should be positively identified as belonging with the spearhead, as it also could have become attached to the twine at any point following the placement of the weapon with the deceased.

8.2 THE WOOD FROM THE SPEARHEAD FROM GRAVE 22 (N. LIPHSCHITZ)

A spearhead, excavated at Gesher in association with Grave 22, was found to have a small wood fragment (ca. 2–3 cm long) still lodged in the tang. The minute sample of wood was a green-blue color, probably as a result of impregnation of the wood from the corroded metal.

The wood sample was treated in absolute ethyl alcohol, dipped in a solution of celloidin in clove oil for 24 hours, rinsed in absolute ethyl alcohol, and finally transferred to 55 C of paraffin, which was then placed in the oven for 96 hours. A block was made from the paraffin. Cross sections and longitudinal, tangential, and radial sections, 12 microns thick, were made with a microtome. Identification of the wood to the species level, based on the three-dimensional structure of the wood, was derived microscopically from these sections.

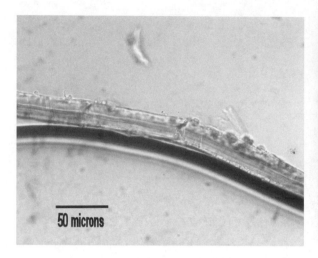

Fig. 8.1 *Fiber 1 at 400× magnification under regular light (photo by A. Gorski).*

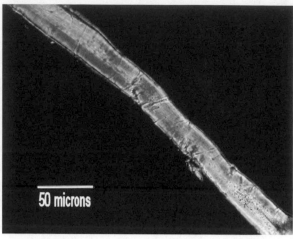

Fig. 8.2 *Fiber 1 at 400× magnification under polarized light (photo by A. Gorski).*

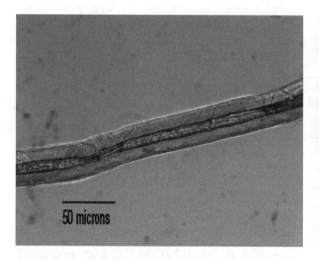

Fig. 8.3 *Fiber 2 at 400× magnification under regular light (photo by A. Gorski).*

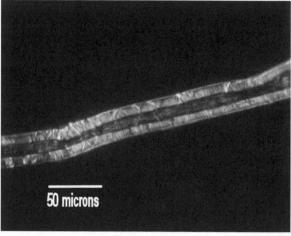

Fig. 8.4 *Fiber 2 at 400× magnification under polarized light (photo by A. Gorski).*

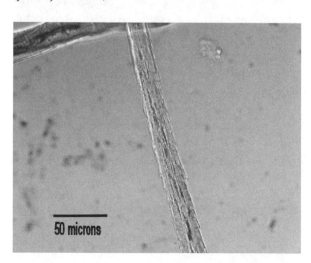

Fig. 8.5 *Animal hair attached to flax fiber at 400× magnification (photo by A. Gorski).*

The sample was compared to reference sections prepared from systematically identified living trees and shrubs, as well as anatomical atlases. The impregnation of the corroded metal into the wood detracted from the accurate identification of the wood species. As could be seen microscopically, however, the wood originated from *Pistacia*, most probably *Pistacia atlantica* (Atlantic pistachio).

Pistacia atlantica is a broad-leaved hardwood species that develops a wide and tall trunk. Its timber is suitable for preparing objects or handles that demand resistant, hard wood. *Pistacia palaestina* trees grow native today and, no doubt, also grew native in antiquity in northern Israel in the Upper and Lower Galilee, the Dan Valley, the Hula Plain, and in the Upper Jordan Valley. Sometimes this species of tree is found in cemeteries (Zohary 1972: 297).

Two alternatives regarding the hafting of the spearhead are possible. One is that the spearhead was made on the site itself, in which case there is no doubt that the wood inserted in the tang of the spearhead originated from a tree that grew in the cemetery or from a tree that grew in the region. The second option is that the spearhead was made in another place and brought to the site.

Chapter 9

The Bone Beverage Strainers

by Aren M. Maeir

9.1 THE OBJECTS

Two unusual bone implements found in the MB IIA graves at Gesher are interpreted as strainers (for beer or wine), similar to the metal strainers reported from various sites throughout the ancient Near East.

The first bone implement (figs. 9.1–2; Item 22 in Table 3.1, p. 58) was discovered in the jar (Item 20) found in association with Grave 7. The bone, which is finely polished, is 5.4 cm long and 1.3–1.4 cm wide.[1] It is hollow and closed only at one extremity. Near the closed end there is a series of nine drilled holes, three on each of the three facets of the bone. The open extremity is broken and, thus, the original length and shape is not fully preserved.

The second bone implement (figs. 9.1, 9.3; Item 21 in Table 3.1, p. 58) was found in Grave 4A. The object was found in the vicinity of the skeleton, while the other associated objects (three pottery bowls) were found some 60 cm above the skull. The implement is 5.8 cm long and 1.8–1.9 cm wide. It is hollow, conical in shape, and has a distinctly triangular cross-section. Both extremities are open, and one can discern that it was intentionally and evenly cut at both sides. The object is polished both inside and out. Near the wider opening there are two holes, while near the narrow opening there is a series of six perforations, two on each facet of the bone.[2]

9.2 DISCUSSION

Three additional perforated hollow bone objects dating to the Middle Bronze Age, with a series of perforations situated usually at one extremity, very similar to the two objects from Gesher, are known from the following sites in Canaan (Maeir and Garfinkel 1992).

SASA: The Kibbutz Sasa local museum exhibits a bone object in the showcase dedicated to Middle Bronze Age II finds from the site. Although there is no information about the exact context of the object, it seems that it was found during modern building activities, which cut into Middle Bronze Age II deposits, as indicated by the archaeological excavations conducted at the site (Bahat 1986: 92). The object is 6 cm long and 1.5 cm wide; it is well polished on the outside and, similar to the object from Gesher, is closed at one extremity (fig. 9.4). Near that extremity are eight perforated holes

119

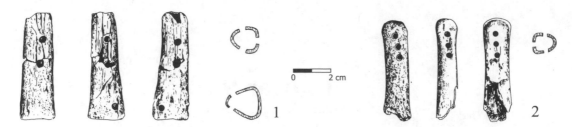

FIG. 9.1   *Drawings of perforated bones from Gesher.*

(three, three, and two on the respective facets). An additional perforated hole is situated near the open extremity.

Kabri: A perforated bone object was found in vicinity of the MB II burials in Area B at Tel Kabri (for a general discussion of these burials, see Scheftelowitz and Gershuny 2002: 29–34). Kishon and Hellwing (1990: 49, fig. 23:3) mention the object in the preliminary report, although they do not suggest a function for it. Surprisingly, the object is not mentioned in any of the various discussions in the recently published final report on the excavations at Kabri (Kempinski 2002). The object, which is 10.5–9.7 cm long, is identified as a left hind metatarsus and is worked and polished. It has six drilled holes near one extremity and one near the other and is very similar to the object from Sasa, save for that it is slightly longer and both extremities are open (although the extremity near the series of six perforations has a very narrow opening).

Megiddo: A bone object, possibly similar to this type was found at Megiddo, near tomb T.3144, which was attributed to stratum XIV of the Middle Bronze Age IIA (Loud 1948: pl. 286:4; Gerstenblith 1983: 27). From the publication it is not clear whether the bone is hollow or not. If it is, there seem to be at least two holes near the open extremity of the bone object and at least four holes near the extremity that seems to be closed.

The findspot of the bone object from Grave 7 at Gesher (inside a jar) serves as a clue to the function of these objects (Maeir and Garfinkel 1992). Small conical perforated metal objects from Bronze and

FIG. 9.2   *Perforated bone (Item 22) from Grave 7.*

FIG. 9.3   *Perforated bone (Item 21) from Grave 4A.*

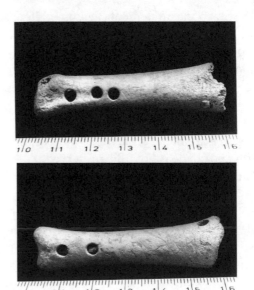

FIG. 9.4   *Perforated bone from Sasa (photo by Howard Smithline).*

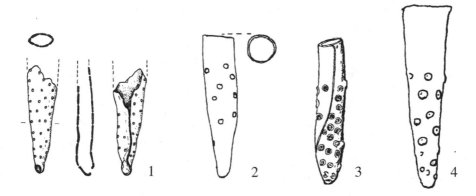

FIG. 9.5   *Metal strainers from various sites. 1: Lachish (Ussishkin 2004: fig. 23:6, 9), 2: Tell el Ajjul (Petrie 1934: pl. 34:423), 3: Gezer (Macalister 1912: 44, fig. 240), 4: Baghouz (du Mesnil du Buisson 1945: pl. 57:Z232).*

Iron Age contexts have been found inside jars at the following sites: Chagar Bazar (Mallowan 1936: 28; 1937: 99), Baghouz (du Mesnil du Buisson 1948: 51–52; Gates 1988: 71; Hrouda 1990: 103), Nippur (Gibson 1988–89: 13–14), and Tell el-Yahudiyeh (Griffith 1890: 46; pl. 15:20–21; Sparks 2004: 38). At Tell el-Yahudiyeh (Sparks 2004: 36, Petrie Museum UC 64827) and Baghouz, straw was found inside the perforated metal objects. In addition to those metal strainers found inside jars, quite a few other examples of such items are known from various Bronze Age Near Eastern contexts (fig. 9.5; Table 9.1). These metal implements have been explained on numerous occasions as strainers, placed at the end of straws, for drinking fermented beverages from a jar (Griffith 1926; du Mesnil du Buisson 1948: 51–52; Engberg 1942: 21; Moorey 1980: 182–83; Ziffer 1990: 84; Simon 1992; Homan 2004: 86; Sparks 2004: 34–35).[3]

This interpretation is corroborated by the iconographic and textual material (fig. 9.6). In the ancient Near Eastern glyptic art there are numerous depictions of people drinking from jars with straws (Hartman and Oppenheim 1950: 12–13; Moorey 1980: 182–83), appearing as early as the mid-fourth millennium BCE (Kantor 1978–79: 35). Du Mesnil du Buisson, who besides the metal strainers found a cylinder seal with such a scene at Baghouz, rightly made the connection between the interpretation of the metal objects as strainers and the scenes on the seals. In addition, he noted

that as in the glyptic art, where one or two drinkers are depicted, one or two strainers were found inside the jars (du Mesnil du Buisson 1948: 51–52).[4] Such cylinder seals have also been found in Israel (Parker 1949: 8, pl. 2:9).

Therefore, in light of these parallels with the metal objects, it is proposed (Maeir and Garfinkel 1992) that the perforated bone implements are, in fact, similar strainers that were originally placed on straws and used for drinking. This would explain why the implement from Grave 7 at Gesher was found inside a jar.[5] Likewise, the function of the holes near the closed or narrow extremity would be for straining the fluids, while the hole(s) on the other side would serve to fasten the straw to the bone. They may very well be a "poor man's" strainer, functioning similarly to the metal counterparts. The relatively large size of the holes in the bone objects, as well as their relatively small number compared to the metal parallels, may hinder the use of the bone objects as strainers (since the holes could be easily blocked by the larger sediment particles in the beverage). Perhaps a solution to this problem would be to wrap a piece of cloth around the bone implement to block the large particles of sediments from reaching the strainer.[6]

The MB IIA burials at Gesher are quite reminiscent of EB IV/MB I mortuary customs, while at the same time incorporating new MB IIA objects and traditions (Maeir 1997a: 215; Garfinkel 2001: 157). In fact, it has been suggested (Maeir 1997a;

TABLE 9.1 Metal strainers found in Bronze and Iron Age contexts in the ancient Near East.

REGION	SITE	DATE	QTY	REFERENCE
EGYPT	Gurob	Late Bronze	5	Petrie 1917: 38; Thomas 1981: 69
	Koptos	Late Bronze	2	Petrie 1917: 38
	El-Amarna	Late Bronze	1	Griffith 1926: fig. 1
	Unknown	Late Bronze	?	Radwan 1983: 164; Sparks 2004: 35
ISRAEL	Tell el-Ajjul	Middle Bronze	2	Petrie 1934: pl. 32.423; Petrie et al. 1952: 15, pl. 16: 201
	Anthedon	Late Bronze/ Iron Age	1	Petrie 1937: 9, pl. 19.59
	Gezer	Middle Bronze ?	1	Macalister 1912: 44
	Megiddo	Middle Bronze	1	Loud 1948: pl. 190:14
	Lachish	Late Bronze	1	Sass 2004: fig. 23.6:9
SYRIA	Alalakh	Late Bronze	12	Woolley 1955: 281, 284, pl. 73.8, 26
	Tell Brak	Middle Bronze	2	Philip 1997: 116, figs. 144, 235:61–63
	Tell Brak	Late Bronze	1	Philip 1997: 116; figs. 144, 235:61–63
	T. Munbaqa	Late Bronze	36	Czichon and Werner 1998: 92, nos. 826–861; Werner 1998: 79, fig. 100
	Meskene-Emar	Late Bronze	?	Beyer 1982: 119, fig. 1; Magueron 1975: 72
	Hammam et-Turkman	Late Bronze	?	de Feyter 1988: 611; pl. 190.7–9
	T. Halawa	Late Bronze	1	Meyer and Pruss 1994: 249, fig. 75.61
TURKEY	Norşuntepe	Late Bronze	2	Schmidt 2002: 55–56, tbl. 51.682–83
IRAQ	Tell Makhmur	Iron Age	1	El-Amin and Mallowan 1950: 56, 68
IRAN	Tepe-Giyan	Middle Bronze ?	1	Contenau and Ghirshman 1935: 47, pl. 35

2002) that this is perhaps to be seen as evidence of the transitional nature of these burials and of the early MB IIA culture in the Jordan Valley in general. This region was somewhat peripheral during the early MB IIA and did not play a major role in the nascent changes occurring at this time, changes which are seen primarily along the coastal plain and in the Jezreel Valley (Gerstenblith 1980: 115–19; Cohen 2002a: 123–28, 137). It would seem that during the early MB IIA in the Jordan valley, there was on the one hand a continuity of earlier EB IV/MB I traditions, while at the same time a partial percolation of some of the new cultural aspects occurred.

As far as the drinking habits and ceremonies as seen from the Gesher burials are concerned, it would appear that those of the MB IIA were adopted and those of the earlier EB IV/MB I were rejected. The drinking habits and ceremonies of the EB IV/MB I are typified by a proliferation of goblets, apparently emulating drinking customs originating in Syria (Bunimovitz and Greenberg 2004). It would seem that the community that buried its dead at Gesher during the early MB IIA had re-oriented its emulatory focus, vis-à-vis its drinking customs, implementing a new custom previously unknown in the region. As suggested regarding the EB IV/MB I, this custom may have also originated in Syria (as seen in the burials at Baghouz) but was clearly of a very different nature than the older custom.

Changes in the dietary/drinking habits can be noticed in the transition between EB IV/MB I and MB IIA. Zooarchaeological studies have noted changes in the preferences and types of animals that were slaughtered for consumption, as well as identified an apparent rise in the use of milk and milk products during the MB II (Clutton-Brock

1971: 43; Horwitz 1989: 51; 2001b: 116; Grigson 1995: 257). At the same time, archaeobotanical studies indicate the appearance of new types of plant-derived foods during this period (Kislev et al. 1993) and a preference for barley (Hopf 1983: 579).[7]

These changes are also evident in the pottery repertoire. As mentioned above, while during the EB IV/MB I the goblet played a major role in the pottery repertoire, this is not seen in the MB IIA. It can be suggested that during the MB II, it was customary to drink directly from small jars or from the various jugs common during this period. It may very well be that one of the reasons of the appearance and development of jars with rounded and eventually pointed bottoms was to enable sediments to settle, which would facilitate drinking beverages from a jar with a straw, thus picking up smaller amounts of sediment.

The appearance of bone straw-tip strainers in the MB IIA graves at Gesher is indicative of various aspects of early MB IIA society in the Jordan Valley. It seems that the appearance of these objects both at Gesher and at other MB II sites is to be related to other changes that occurred during this period throughout Canaan, changes that affected a wide

FIG. 9.6 *Drinking scenes on Mesopotamian cylinder seals, with one or two persons (Amiet 1960: pl. 89:1166, 1171).*

range of cultural facets. In addition, the fact that these items were made of bone and not of the more standard metal, is an additional indication of the peripheral nature of the early MB IIA settlement in this region.

NOTES

1 The bone is mammalian but no further species identification was possible.

2 The bone was identified as a fragment of the tibia shaft of a small to medium mammal – possibly sheep/goat or gazelle.

3 An initial interpretation of this object as a rasp (Griffith 1890: 46; Petrie 1917: 38) is still adhered to by Thomas (1981: 69).

4 Similar scenes are found in New Kingdom Egyptian material (Griffith 1926; Vandier d'Abbadie 1937). From the cuneiform textual material, there is mention of both the straws (*ša mē šūli/šulpu*) and the strainers (*šūlû*) that were used for drinking (Salonen 1965: 44–46).

5 A possible explanation as to why many of these strainers (bone and metal) were not found in jars is that many of the receptacles for brewing and serving beer were of perishable materials (Civil 1964:

87) and, thus, only the strainers survived the post-depositional processes.

6 It should be noted that the implements from Grave 4A at Gesher and from Kabri are open at both extremities, which would seem to be unsuitable for a strainer. It is possible that the narrow extremity of the objects may have served as an additional straining hole due to its small size (as with the object from Kabri) or could have been blocked up during use. It must also be considered, however, that these objects could belong to a different class of bone objects.

7 For comparison, one can note that substantial changes in the dietary practices in ancient Egypt are seen during both the Middle Kingdom and the New Kingdom (Murray 2000: 610, tbl. 2.4.1; Ikram 2001: 293–94), most likely due to various external influences (e.g., trade and other contacts) but possibly due to economic reasons as well.

Chapter 10

The Faunal Remains

by Liora Kolska Horwitz

10.1 INTRODUCTION

The majority of Middle Bronze Age II (MB II) tombs in the southern Levant have yielded a rich corpus of material culture comprising ceramic vessels, ornaments, weapons, and other artifacts crafted from bronze, stone, and bone (Hallote 1995; Ilan 1995; 1996; Maeir 1997b; Garfinkel 2001; Gonen 2001), including faunal remains. It has been suggested (Horwitz 2001a) that the animal remains were intentionally introduced as funerary offerings and probably represent symbolic features of the Middle Bronze Age belief system – gifts for the gods, ritual food for the deceased and/or the community, a substitute for human beings, a commemoration of the deceased, a symbol of life and, hence, the conquest of death, or a sign of a covenant with the gods and/or the deceased. This report provides information on fauna recovered from five MB IIA graves in the Gesher cemetery, representing further examples of mortuary offerings in this period.

10.2 THE FAUNA

Grave 4B

Grave 4B was a single, primary burial that was overlain by another interment (Grave 4A). Grave goods found with the skeleton in Grave 4B were a jar and juglet placed near the head, and a bowl located near the knees. On the ground adjacent to the head, a group of animal bones was found, identified as fragmented rib shafts of a medium-sized mammal, probably sheep/goat (Table 10.1).

Grave 10

This grave contained remains of two human skeletons, probably not interred at the same time. Burial goods comprised a variety of ceramic vessels placed near the upper thorax/abdomen area of the skeletons. A bowl was found containing twenty-five highly fragmented bones, some of which might be human, and one bone that was identifiable as a rib

TABLE 10.1 Sheep/goat remains (NISP counts) listed by grave and skeletal element.

TOMB/VESSEL	GRAVE 4B	GRAVE 10 BOWL	GRAVE 13	GRAVE 21 JAR #3	GRAVE 21 BOWL #4	GRAVE 23 BOWL #6
Species	?sheep/goat	?sheep/goat	sheep	?sheep/goat	sheep/goat	sheep
Side of Skeleton	undet.	undet.	right	undet.	(?left)	left
Age	undet.	juvenile	< 2 years	undet.	< 3 years	≥ 3.5 years
MNI estimate	1	1	1	1	1	1
SKELETAL ELEMENT			FORELIMB			
dist. scapula	–	–	–	–	–	1
dist. humerus	–	–	–	–	1 •	1
humerus shaft	–	–	–	–	–	1
radius shaft	–	–	–	–	1 •	–
carpal	–	–	–	–	1 •	–
			HINDLIMB			
pelvis	–	–	–	–	–	1
prox. femur	–	–	–	–	–	1
femur shaft	–	–	1 *	–	1	–
dist. femur	–	–	–	–	–	1
patella	–	–	–	–	–	1
prox. tibia	–	–	–	–	–	1
tibia shaft	–	–	1	–	1	–
dist. tibia	–	–	–	–	–	1
navicullo-cuboid	–	–	1	–	–	–
prox. calcaneus	–	–	–	–	1	–
dist. calcaneus	–	–	1	–	–	–
calcaneus whole	–	–	–	–	–	1
astragalus	–	–	1	–	–	–
tarsal	–	–	–	–	–	1
			FOOT			
phalanx	–	–	–	–	1	–
			TRUNK			
prox. rib	–	–	–	–	–	3
rib shaft frags.	3	1	–	1	–	28
TOTAL NISP	3	1	5	1	7	42

Key to the table:
undet.: undetermined
MNI: Minimum Number of Individuals
NISP: Number of Identified Specimens

• found immediately outside Bowl 4
* This bone was incorrectly identified as a humerus shaft in Horwitz and Garfinkel 1991.

fragment of a medium-sized (juvenile?) mammal, possibly sheep/goat. It is possible that these remains were not intentionally placed in the vessel but form accidental inclusions from the sediment.

Grave 13

This grave has been identified as a warrior grave since it contained remains of a primary human burial lying in a semi-flexed position, together with a bronze duckbill axe and a bronze spearhead. A jar and a bowl were the only ceramic vessels found. The animal remains were found on the ground to the north of the skull (see fig. 3.54 in Chapter 3). They were lying in partial anatomical association and comprised bones from the right hindlimb (femur, tibia, navicullo-cuboid, calcaneus, astragulus). Based on the morphology of the complete astragalus they were identified as sheep, *Ovis aries* (Boessneck 1969; Prummel and Frisch 1986). The animal was immature and aged less than two years since the distal tibia was still unfused (Silver 1969).

Grave 21

This was a single interment of a female. There was a broken storage jar placed at her feet containing bones, while animal remains were also found inside an open bowl situated in the area of the thorax (chest; fig. 10.1).

The storage jar yielded eight unidentified bone fragments (all less than 2mm in length), some of which might be human, and a small fragment of rib from a medium-sized mammal. It is unclear whether these remains were intentionally placed in the pot or represent accidental inclusions from the soil matrix. In contrast, the animal remains recovered from the open bowl (Item 79) appear to have been intentionally placed there. They comprise thirty-two unidentified small fragments (2 mm in length or smaller), seven larger unidentified fragments (2–5 mm in length), and four identified bones from the hindlimb (femur, tibia, calcaneus, phalanx), probably the left side, of a sheep/goat. The animal was aged on the basis of an unfused

FIG. 10.1 *Open bowl containing animal remains from Grave 21.*

proximal calcaneus epiphysis as less than three years old (Silver 1969). In the area immediately around the open bowl, three fragmented bones from the upper forelimb (humerus, radius, carpal) of a sheep/goat were found that probably belong to the animal in the bowl.

Grave 23

This context yielded a complete, extended primary burial, probably of an adult male. Grave goods comprised ceramic vessels, including a bowl containing animal remains. The vessel had been placed in the region of the upper thorax and abdomen of the deceased (fig. 10.2).

This bowl contained forty-two bones representing the left upper forelimb (scapula, humerus), left hindlimb (pelvis, femur, patella, tibia, calcaneus, tarsal), and trunk (proximal ribs and rib shafts) of an adult sheep (*Ovis aries*) identified on the basis of morphology of the distal scapula, distal humerus, proximal femur, distal tibia, and calcaneus (Boessneck 1969; Prummel and Frisch 1986). The animal was aged at least three and a half years, due to the presence of a fused distal femur and proximal tibia, which are fully fused by this time (Silver 1969).

10.3 Discussion

A total of twenty-three tombs were excavated at Gesher, but only five graves (twenty-four percent) yielded animal offerings (Graves 4, 10, 13, 19, and 22). Each of these graves contained remains of one animal associated with a single human interment, indicating a direct association between the number of animal offerings and the deceased. The presence of offerings in selected graves may be an indication of the social status of the interred.

The animal bones from Gesher were all found in close association with the human remains and the other grave offerings. In four instances, bones were found inside ceramic vessels (Grave 10: a bowl; Grave 21: a storage jar and a bowl; Grave 23: a bowl), suggesting that meat offerings may have been cooked or at least were intended to resemble a prepared dish of food when placed in the tomb. At Jericho, there were two instances of animal remains associated with wooden containers (Tombs J3 and L7), which led Grosvenor Ellis and Westley (1965) to suggest that in instances where bones were found scattered without a container, the container had probably disintegrated.

No burnt animal bones were found in the Gesher sample nor in the other MB IIA tomb assemblages studied by Horwitz (2001a). This does not necessarily mean that raw meat was used for offerings, since boiling, baking, or even grilling may not necessarily leave signs on the bones (Binford 1972; Pearce and Luff 1994). Similarly, no butchery damage was evident on any of the bones in the Gesher sample.

In two instances at Gesher (Graves 4B and 13), the animal remains had been placed near the head of the deceased on the ground, while in three cases they were placed in bowls on or near the upper thorax/abdomen (Graves 10, 21, and 23). A similar example is found in the MB II Tomb 3004 at Tel Dan, where animal bones were found on the thorax/abdomen of the interred (Horwitz 1996a), while at Jericho (Tomb G42) they were described as having been placed near the hands (Grosvenor Ellis and Westley 1965: 697). These features emphasize that the animal bones represent food items placed conveniently close to the deceased's mouth or hands, as if they were intended for consumption.

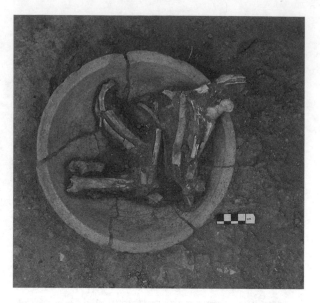

Fig. 10.2 *Open bowl containing animal remains from Grave 23.*

It is difficult to determine whether the Gesher animal remains were in full or partial anatomical connection, since in most cases they had been placed in ceramic vessels, which has masked their original association. The fact that in three cases the bones found in a single locality all derive from the same side of the skeleton and follow anatomical sequence (Table 10.1) suggests that they were introduced as joints. They probably still had meat or at least ligaments adhering, which served to maintain their association. Cornwall (1965) and Grosvenor Ellis and Westley (1965) reported that at Jericho bones were found in anatomical association, especially ribs and vertebrae.

There is some degree of inter-site variation in the limb elements represented in MB II tomb assemblages. In most cases, such as Hazor (Horwitz 1997) and Tel Dan (Horwitz 1996a), there is evidence for intentional selection of upper limbs and trunk elements, which are rich in meat. In this regard, the skeletal elements found at Gesher represent meat-rich limbs or trunk elements. At Jericho, the inverse appears to be true (Cornwall 1965; Grosvenor Ellis and Westley 1965: 700–701). Common to all MB II sites is the absence or paucity of cranial remains (including teeth) and foot bones (phalanges). The absence of teeth is of special note, given that they are the most robust elements in the skeleton. These two body part categories may have been selectively disposed of at the primary slaughter locality, since, aside from the brain, they are relatively poor in meat.

In most Middle Bronze Age tombs that have been studied to date, there is evidence for the preferential selection of young caprines (Horwitz 2001a). The same pattern is observed at Gesher, where three of the four animals that could be aged were less than three years old.

At Gesher, of the remains that could be identified to species, at least two were sheep (Graves 13 and 23). In Grave 21, an unidentified sheep/goat is represented, while in Graves 4B and 10 the undetermined medium-size mammal probably represents a sheep/goat. The preference for caprines, and especially sheep, may also be observed in other Middle Bronze Age tombs. It probably reflects a general economic trend in the region relating to wool production, since at this time sheep dominate the caprine assemblages from domestic sites (Horwitz 2001a).

It has been postulated (Horwitz 2001a) that in the preceding MB I (EB IV), tomb offerings were limited to a few taxa, primarily sheep and goat, while in the MB II this was expanded to include a richer and more diverse range of species (equids, deer, birds, fish). The absence of remains other than caprines in the MB IIA tombs at Gesher and Hazor, dated to the MB IIA–B (Horwitz 1997), would seem to negate this idea. However, it is possible that there exists a chronological distinction between phases of the MB II, with caprines having been exclusively exploited as offerings in the earlier phases (MB IIA–B), as at Yoqneam (Horwitz et al. 2005), Hazor (Horwitz 1997), and Gesher. In contrast, tombs with a more varied species range, such as Sasa (Horwitz 1987; 1996b) and Tel Dan (Horwitz 1996a), span all three phases of this period (MB IIA–C). A possible exception are the MB I/MB IIA tombs at Efrat (Horwitz 2001b). The ten tombs excavated at Efrat are all dominated by sheep/goat remains. However, five of the ten tombs have additionally yielded bones (albeit in small numbers) of cattle, pig, and donkey (Horwitz 2001b: tbl. 7.3). The other non-caprine remains may represent more recent inclusions (carnivores, birds, rodents, and reptiles). Further tomb assemblages are required to investigate this hypothesis.

10.4   CONCLUSIONS

At Gesher, the recovered animal bones represent remains of food offerings, selected for species and age, that have been intentionally placed in the tombs. In some instances, ceramic vessels were used for storing these offerings (placed on or near the deceased), while in others they were placed on the ground near the interred. It is possible that articulated joints of meat had been introduced, given the fact that bones from the same side of the skeleton and limb are found, many in primary connection. Primarily remains of immature caprines, especially those of sheep, were recovered. It may be concluded then that the MB II tomb fauna is characterized by a narrower range of species and age classes than that from coeval secular sites. These features place Gesher within the general pattern observed for contemporaneous mortuary assemblages. They represent the continuation of a mortuary tradition that may have begun as early as the Early Bronze Age, as attested to by fauna from the tombs at Bab edh-Dhra (Hesse and Wapnish 1981) and Horbat Zelef (R. Kehati pers. comm. 2005).

Chapter 11

Gesher in MB IIA Context

by Susan Cohen

11.1 INTRODUCTION

The site of Gesher has considerable significance for both mortuary and cultural studies of MB IIA development in Canaan. Located as it is in the central Jordan valley, Gesher, its burials, and the material culture excavated at the site present an opportunity to examine the beginning of MB IIA in an area removed from the coastal regions and the characteristics of urbanized MB IIA culture so readily apparent there. The site provides a window into the transition from EB IV/MB I and the nature of the earliest phases of MB IIA. To assess its importance in this role, three aspects will be discussed further below: 1) the potential nature of the settlement related to the cemetery, 2) other MB IIA mortuary sites in Canaan in comparison with Gesher, and 3) the transition between EB IV/MB I and MB IIA as illustrated by the cemetery at Gesher.

11.2 GESHER AND MB IIA SETTLEMENT

It is notable that no settlement has yet been discovered in relation to the cemetery at Gesher. While several small early MB IIA settlements exist in the Jordan valley region (fig. 11.1), such as

Tell el-Hayyat (Falconer and Magness-Gardiner 1984), Tell Kitan (Eisenberg 1993), and Kfar Rupin (Gophna 1979), these sites are either not located close enough to Gesher to make it seem feasible for their inhabitants to have utilized the cemetery, or else date far later in the Middle Bronze Age than Gesher. It is possible that the settlement, if there was one, is located under the alluvia of the nearby Jordan valley plains and has not yet been located, or that is has been destroyed by modern activities and build-up in the region. Given Gesher's proximity to the modern border, it is also possible that the associated settlement is located in regions inaccessible for survey and excavation.[1]

Another factor to be taken into consideration when examining the problem of associated settlement, is the character of the cemetery itself. As discussed further below, some of the features of the interments found at Gesher are traditionally considered typical of less sedentary populations; the cemetery may have been utilized seasonally and may not have been associated with a permanent settlement.[2] This phenomenon is common throughout the preceding EB IV/MB I period in Canaan, and it is possible that Gesher reflects a continuation of this trend.

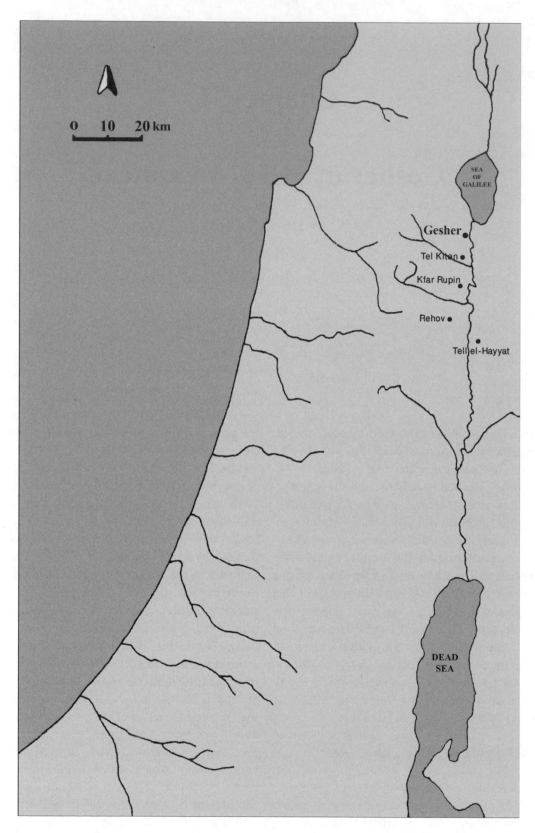

FIG. 11.1 *Map showing MB IIA settlement sites in the Gesher region.*

11.3   Burial Sites in MB IIA:
A Comparison with Gesher

In addition to Gesher, other MB IIA cemetery sites without an associated settlements have been found throughout Canaan (fig. 11.2). Of these sites, few show many similarities with Gesher beyond some basic parallels within the assemblage of material culture as a whole. The list below presents a brief description of these other burial sites (Table 11.1), together with a comparison of these sites with Gesher.[3]

Afula

Six burials excavated at Afula, numbers 3, 11–14, and 19, date to MB IIA (Sukenik 1948). The pottery from these tombs, including a juglet fragment with a triple-stranded handle and a juglet with a "candle-stick" rim, is typical of the later phases of MB IIA (Cohen 2002a); overall, the associated material culture dates much later than the assemblage from Gesher. Little information is available regarding the skeletal material and interments.

'Ain es-Samiyeh

The MB IIA remains from this site utilized previously hewn EB IV/MB I shaft tombs. Nine MB IIA vessels, including an open bowl with a ring-base, a piriform juglet, a handleless jar, and forms with red slip and burnish (Dever 1975: 31), as well as a fenestrated duckbilled axehead, two socketed spearheads, and a ribbed dagger were found in the tombs. The weapon assemblage is typically MBIIA (Oren 1971: 113; Philip 1989: 49) and has some parallels with the weapons found at Gesher; the ceramic material has fewer parallels and dates later in the MB IIA chronological sequence of development (Cohen 2002a).

Beth Shan

The weapon assemblage in Tomb 92 included a duckbill axe, a socketed spearhead, a ribbed dagger, and other artifacts (Oren 1973: fig. 24:12–16). The assemblage has a clear MB IIA date and is consis-tent with the weapon assemblage from Gesher. No pottery was found in the tomb, and there is little information available regarding the nature of the burials themselves.

Efrata

The Middle Bronze Age burials at this site reused cave tombs hewn in the preceding EB IV/MB I (Gonen 2001). Multiple burials were associated with each cave, in contrast to the single primary interments at Gesher. The ceramic assemblage is consistent with a date in late MB IIA or the transitional period from MB IIA to IIB (Gonen 2001) and, thus, dates considerably later than Gesher.

Gibeon

At least two of the EB IV/MB I shaft tombs at this site were reused during MB IIA. Remains from this period include a two-handled store-jar (Pritchard 1963: fig. 34:1), flat-based handleless jars (Pritchard 1963: fig. 64:9–11), and spearheads (Pritchard 1963: fig. 64:12–13). Overall, the assemblage indicates a date in early to mid-MB IIA (Gerstenblith 1983: 34–35; Cohen 2002a; 2002b). Few parallels exist between material from Gibeon and Gesher.

Hagosherim

Two of the three burial caves at this site have material dating to MB IIA; the ceramic assemblage includes Levantine Painted Ware, carinated bowls, and ovoid handleless store-jars, all of which indicate an early MB IIA date (Covello-Paran 1996; Cohen 2002a; 2002b). Three bronze toggle pins were also found in one of the caves. There are several parallels between the Hagosherim assemblage and that found at Gesher, many of which have been noted in the discussion of the ceramic typology and specific vessels in Chapter 5.

Kefar Szold

The assemblage from this tomb is typical of the transitional MB IIA–IIB period (Cohen 2002a; Epstein 1974) and includes such characteristic

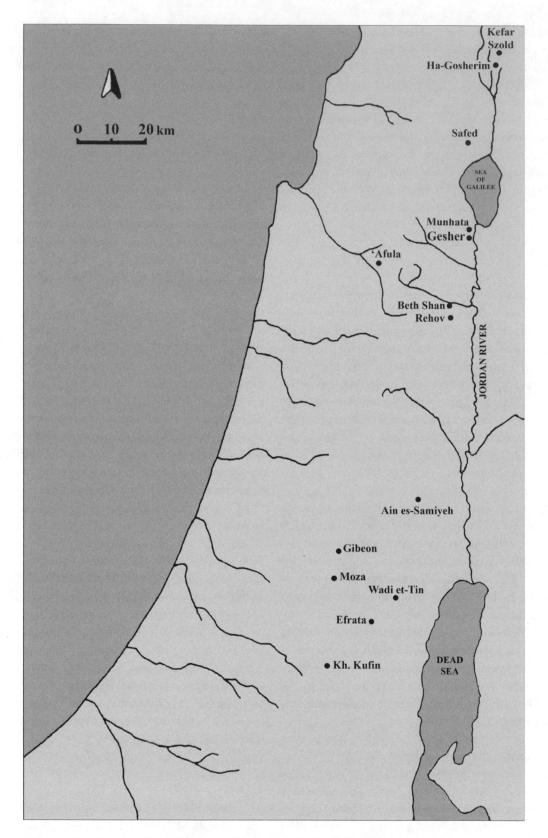

FIG. 11.2 *Map showing other MB IIA mortuary sites in inland and/or peripheral regions.*

Table 11.1 List of mortuary sites without associated settlements.

Site Name	Coordinates	Date in MB IIA	References
Afula	177, 224	Late MB IIA	Sukenik 1948
Ain es-Samiyeh	181, 155	Middle MB IIA	Dever 1975
Beth Shan	197, 212	Mid-MB IIA	Oren 1971
Efrata	164, 117	MB IIA–IIB transition	Gonen 2001
Gibeon	167, 139	Early–Mid MB IIA	Pritchard 1963
Hagosherim	208, 291	Early MB IIA	Covello-Paran 1996
Kfar Szold	211, 288	MB IIA–IIB transition	Epstein 1974
Khirbet Kufin	160, 114	Middle MB IIA	Smith 1962
Moza	165, 133	MB IIA–IIB transition	Sussman 1966
Munhata	202, 225	Late MB IIA	Ferembach et al. 1975
Rehov	197, 207	Early MB IIA	Yogev 1985
Safed	197, 263	MB IIA–IIB transition	Damati and Stepansky 1996
Wadi et-Tin	171, 122	Mid–Late MB IIA	Vincent 1947

forms as a piriform juglet with a double- or triple-stranded handle and "candlestick" rim, and large deep burnished bowls with rounded carination (Epstein 1974: 2–3, figs. 1.1, 3.6–8). This tomb dates much later than the cemetery at Gesher and does not provide accurate comparative material.

Khirbet Kufin

One tomb of this large cemetery site was reused during MB IIA (Smith 1962), and the ceramics from this tomb fit well with the middle phases of the MB IIA period (Cohen 2002a; 2002b). There are no close parallels with the Gesher materials.

Moza

Three intact shaft tombs were excavated at this site. While the majority of the ceramics were predominately MB IIB, some forms may date to MB IIA (Sussman 1966: 42; fig. 2). A notched socket axe may also be an MB IIA form. Overall, the tombs date to the transitional MB IIA-IIB period with continued use in MB IIB. There are no close comparisons that may be made with the cemetery at Gesher.

Munhata

The ceramics from a group of tombs at this site include bowls with high rounded carination (Ferembach et al. 1975: fig. 3), and a juglet with a stepped rim (Ferembach et al. 1975: fig. 5), typical of the MB IIA–IIB transitional period. The material from this site dates considerably later than that from Gesher, although many of the bowls are similar to the Gesher assemblage in their uneven and lopsided stances (see, for example, Ferembach et al. 1975: fig 2). Despite its geographical proximity to Gesher, there are no close parallels between the typology of the assemblages at the two sites, nor in the methods of interment (Ferembach et al. 1975: 113–17).

Rehov

Shaft tombs south of Tel Rehov yielded MB IIA pottery dating early in the ceramic sequence, including a small handleless jar and a store-jar with a combed band on the shoulder (Yogev 1985: 99). The weapons found in the tombs, including a duckbilled axe and two spearheads (Yogev 1985: fig. 4), also date typologically to MB IIA. Both the weapons and some of the ceramics are comparable with the Gesher material.

Safed

A burial cave dating to very late MB IIA and the MB IIA–IIB transition period was excavated at this site. Twenty complete vessels and fifty bronze weapons, including duckbilled axes, spearheads, and daggers were found in the tomb (Damati and Stepansky 1996). Little information is available regarding the number or nature of the skeletal remains. Other than the weapon typology, there are few parallels with Gesher.

Wadi et-Tin

Some of the ceramics from this cemetery show MB IIA characteristics (Gerstenblith 1983: 34; Vincent 1947). In general, the majority of the ceramics from this site dates much later in MB IIA than the assemblage from Gesher. There are few comparisons that may be made between the two sites.

As can be seen from the site descriptions above, there are few similarities between the cemetery excavated at Gesher and other mortuary sites not closely associated with large urban settlements. The closest parallels in material culture are from Hagosherim and Rehov, which is in keeping with the proximity of those sites to Gesher. Other nearby sites, however, such as Munhata and Afula, show fewer parallels in both method of interment and material culture; this may likely be attributed to the fact that these sites date later in MB IIA than Gesher and, as such, are not directly comparable. The paucity of close parallels to the Gesher cemetery, together with the phenomenon of the single primary interments as found at Gesher, in contrast to the multiple burials at many of these other sites, highlights the early nature of the material culture at the site and its significance for illustrating the transition from EB IV/MB I to MB IIA.

11.4   GESHER AND THE EB IV/MB I–MB IIA TRANSITION

As noted previously, few sites to date provide evidence regarding the transitional period from EB IV/MB I–MB IIA. Excavations at Tell el-Hayyat uncovered material in stratified contexts dating to both EB IV and MB IIA, including a stratum of mixed deposits showing continuity between the two periods (Hayyat Phase 5; Falconer 1985; 1995; Falconer and Magness-Gardiner 1984). Additional early material, potentially reflective of this transition period, was found in the pre-palace phases at Aphek (Beck 1985). Significantly, the evidence from both sites is limited to sherd evidence only; no architectural remains, whole vessels, or other evidence can be attributed to this early phase. The evidence from the burials and associated material culture at Gesher, which was found undisturbed in its original context, therefore, provides valuable data concerning the nature of this transitional period.

It has been frequently suggested that mortuary sites without associated settlements are representative of less complex groups, as opposed to multiple interments and/or cave sites, which are then associated with more sedentary populations and ones with less egalitarian structures (Hallote 1995; Ilan 1995). If so, then it may be suggested that the Gesher cemetery was used by a mostly egalitarian population and perhaps one that traveled seasonally in the region around the site, possibly to access the variety of resources available there (Maeir 1997a: 216). With the exception of the bronze weapons and the toggle pin (Grave 5), there is little evidence for social stratification in the Gesher burials as revealed by the extant associated material culture. This, combined with the early chronological locus of the material culture, may help to reveal the population that used Gesher as illustrative of an "incipient, non-urban stage of the MBIIa" (Maeir 1997a: 216) or, in other words, the period of transition between EB IV/MB I and MB IIA.

In addition, EB IV/MB I burials are often characterized by single interments (Prag 1974; Dever 1987; Hallote 1995), while multiple burials become the more standard method of interment in the Middle Bronze Age. At Gesher, with one exception (Grave 10), all of the burials in the cemetery are single burials in simple graves, as opposed to the more complex multiple interments found elsewhere in MB IIA. Even at those other sites where MB IIA burials utilized earlier shaft tombs, such as 'Ain es-Samiyeh and Efrata, the MB IIA remains consisted of multiple interments rather than the single burials uncovered at Gesher. At Jericho, only two single burials were found, an infant burial and a burial described as a "young warrior;" significantly, both of these burials dated early in the sequence (Kenyon 1960: 264).

The secondary burials at Gesher also have antecedents in the preceding period, as the practice, while common in EB IV/MB I, disappears in the Middle Bronze Age (Ilan 1995: 133; Hallote 1994; 1995).[4] Further, as noted in Chapter 3, the custom of the warrior burial is rooted in the earlier period and becomes gradually less common as the Middle Bronze Age progresses (Hallote 1995; Philip 1989). The seven warrior burials at Gesher also provide a link to earlier traditions (Garfinkel 2001; see also Chapter 3). Even the weapons found with these burials are technologically consistent with earlier practices, as opposed to the more standardized composition of MB IIA weapons (see Chapter 7). Finally, the presence of the faunal offerings in the graves may be viewed as a continuation of earlier practices as well (see Chapter 10); it has been suggested that the prevalence of food-related offerings and grave goods continues to decline in the later phases of the Middle Bronze Age (Hallote 1995: 114–15).

Notably, however, at the same time as the actual methods of interments show affinities with earlier EB IV/MB I customs, the material culture from the cemetery is clearly of MB IIA character. Despite the differences from the standard assemblages for MB IIA as defined by the urban and coastal sites, the characteristics of both the ceramic corpus and the bronze weapons from Gesher are immediately recognizable as MB IIA. In contrast, there are few similarities, if any, with the material cultural traditions from the preceding period.

11.5   CONCLUSIONS

The MB IIA cemetery at Gesher reflects patterns and characteristics of both EB IV/MB I and MB IIA. The material excavated at Gesher illustrates a composite social structure in the central Jordan valley region, in which new factors and influences appear but older practices and societal frameworks continue as well (Maeir 1997a; 2002). It is therefore suggested that, rather than viewing EB IV/MB I sites as bridging the gap between the urbanism of the Early and Middle Bronze Ages (Dever 1992: 88), the mix of traditions found at Gesher instead illustrates a transitional EB IV–MB IIA period, evident in the interior of Canaan.

NOTES

1   A recent study by Faust (2005) discusses the organization and social structure of Middle Bronze Age villages in rural Canaan; although none of the settlements listed are viable candidates for being associated with the Gesher cemetery, these sites do provide possible examples of what such a settlement may be like.

2   It should be noted that the poor state of preservation of the skeletal remains precluded conducting any DNA analysis, so no information is available to posit family relations or kinship structure regarding the cemetery, which might otherwise have helped to shed light on the nature of the population that utilized this site for burial.

3   Cemeteries associated with large urban sites lacking MB IIA occupational layers, but with occupation later in the Middle Bronze Age, such as Tell el-'Ajjul, Beth Shemesh, and Tell Far'ah N, or large urban sites with multiple-burial caves such as Jericho and Megiddo, are not directly comparable to Gesher and therefore are not included in the comparison above. An exception is Tomb 92 at Beth Shan, as this site is within the greater regional area under discussion, and the tomb itself may be interpreted as an isolated MB IIA element at the site.

4   However, secondary burials have been found in the Middle Bronze Age cave tombs at Efrata (Gonen 2001), and date considerably later in MB IIA than Gesher.

References

Amiet, P.

1961 *La glyptique mésopotamienne archaique.* Paris: CNRS.

Amiran, R.

1969 *Ancient Pottery in the Holy Land.* Jerusalem: Massada.

1970 *Ancient Pottery of the Holy Land.* New Brunswick, NJ: Rutgers University.

Bahat, D.

1986 The Excavations at Sasa, 1975. Pp. 85–105 in *The Antiquities of the Western Galilee,* ed. M. Yedayah. Tel Aviv: Ministry of Defense (Hebrew).

Baker, J.

2003 The Middle and Late Bronze Age Tomb Complex at Ashkelon, Israel: The Architecture and the Funeral Kit. Unpublished Ph.D. dissertation. Brown University.

Bass, W. M.

1995 *Human Osteology: A Laboratory and Field Manual,* 4th edition. Special Publications 2. Columbia, MO: Missouri Archaeological Society.

Beck, P.

1975 The Pottery of Middle Bronze Age IIA at Tel Aphek. *Tel Aviv* 2: 45–85.

1985 The Middle Bronze Age IIA Pottery from Aphek, 1972–1984: First Summary. *Tel Aviv* 12: 181–203.

2000a Area B: Pottery. Pp. 93–133 in *Aphek-Antipatris I. Excavation of Areas A and B. The 1972-1976 Seasons,* eds. M. Kochavi, P. Beck and E. Yadin. Institute of Archaeology, Tel Aviv University, Monograph Series 19. Tel Aviv: Yass.

2000b Area A: Middle Bronze Age IIA Pottery. Pp. 173–238 in *Aphek-Antipatris I. Excavation of Areas A and B. The 1972–1976 Seasons,* eds. M. Kochavi, P. Beck and E. Yadin. Institute of Archaeology, Tel Aviv University, Monograph Series 19. Tel Aviv: Yass.

2000c The Middle Bronze Age IIA Pottery Repertoire: A Comparative Study. Pp. 239–54 in *Aphek-Antipatris I. Excavation of Areas A and B. The 1972–1976 Seasons,* eds. M. Kochavi, P. Beck, and E. Yadin. Institute of Archaeology, Tel Aviv University, Monograph Series 19. Tel Aviv: Yass.

Begin, Z. B.; Broeker, W.; Buchbinder, B.; Drukman, Y.; Kaufman, A.; Magaritz, M.; and Neev, D.

1985 Dead Sea and Lake Lisan Levels in the Last 30000 Years. A Preliminary Report. *Israel Geological Survey Report* 29/85: 1–18.

Belitzky, S.

1996 The Tectonic Geomorphology of the Lower Jordan Valley – an Active Continental Rift. Unpublished PhD. Hebrew University. Jerusalem (Hebrew, with English abstract).

Ben-Arieh, J.

1965 *The Central Jordan Valley.* Merhavia: Hakibutz Hameuchad (Hebrew).

Ben-Dor, I.

1950 A Middle Bronze Age Temple at Nahariya. *Quarterly of the Department of Antiquities of Palestine* 14: 1–41.

Beyer, D.

1982 *Meskéné-Emar: Dix Ans de Travaux.* Paris: Éditions Recherche sur les Civilisations.

Binford, L.

1972 An Analysis of Cremations from three Michigan Sites. Pp. 373–82 in *An Archaeological Perspective*, ed. L. Binford. New York: Academic.

Biran, A.

1994 *Biblical Dan.* Jerusalem: Israel Exploration Society/Hebrew Union College.

Birmingham, J.

1977 Spectroanalyses of some MBA Metal Objects. *Levant* 9: 115–19.

Boessneck, J.

1969 Osteological Differences Between Sheep (*Ovis aries Linné*) and Goats (*Capra hircus Linné*). Pp. 331–58 in *Science in Archaeology*, 2nd edition, eds. D. Brothwell and E. S. Higgs. London: Thames and Hudson.

Branigan, K.; McKerrell, H.; and Tylecote, R. F.

1976 An Examination of some Palestinian Bronzes. *Journal of the Historical Metallurgy Society* 10, no. 1: 15–23.

Bucholz, H.-G., and Drescher, H.

1987 Einige frühe Metallgeräte aus Anatolien. *Acta Praehistorica et Archaeologica* 19: 37–70.

Bunimovitz, S., and Greenberg, R.

2004 Revealed in their Cups: Syrian Drinking Customs in Intermediate Bronze Age Canaan. *Bulletin of the American Schools of Oriental Research* 334: 19–31.

Civil, M.

1964 A Hymn to the Beer Goddess and a Drinking Song. Pp. 67–89 in *Studies Presented to A. Leo Oppenheim.* Chicago, IL: Oriental Institute.

Clutton-Brock, J.

1971 The Primary Food Animals of the Jericho Tell from the Proto-Neolithic to the Byzantine Period. *Levant* 3: 41–55.

Cohen, S. L.

2002a *Canaanites, Chronology, and Connections: The Relationship of Middle Bronze Age IIA Canaan to Middle Kingdom Egypt.* Harvard Semitic Museum Publications, Studies in the History and Archaeology of the Levant 3, Winona Lake, IN: Eisenbrauns.

2002b MB IIA Settlement and Ceramic Typology in the Southern Levant. Pp. 113–31 in *The Middle Bronze Age in the Levant. Proceedings of an International Conference on MB IIA Ceramic Material, Vienna, 24th–26th of January, 2001*, ed. M. Bietak. Wien: Österreichische Akademie der Wissenschaften.

2003a Gesher – 2002 (G-77/2002). *Excavations and Surveys in Israel* 115: 28–29, 35.

2003b Gesher Excavations, 2003. *Israel Exploration Journal* 53: 229–32.

2004a Gesher Excavations, 8 June–7 July, 2003. *Excavations and Surveys in Israel* 116: 11–12.

2004b Gesher, 2004. *Israel Exploration Journal* 54: 236–39.

2005 The Spearheads from the 2002–2004 Excavations at Gesher. *Israel Exploration Journal* 55: 129–42.

Contenau, G., and Ghirshman, R.

1935 *Fouilles du Tépé-Giyan près de Nehavend 1931 et 1932: Sondage du Tépé-Djamshidi, Sondage du Tépé-Bad-Hora, 1933, par R. Ghirshman.* Paris: Geuthner.

Cornwall, I. W.

1965 Appendix K (ii). Collections of Animal Bones from Tombs of EB–MB Outsize Type. Pp. 702–3 in *Excavations at Jericho II*, ed. K. M. Kenyon. London: British School of Archaeology in Jerusalem.

Covello-Paran, K.

1996 Middle Bronze Age Burial Caves at Hagosherim, Upper Galilee. *ʾAtiqot* 30: 71–83.

Czichon, R. M., and Werner, P.

1998   Tall Munbāqa – Ekalte I. Die bronzezeitlichen Kleinfunde. Wissenschaftliche Veröffentlichungen der Deutschen Orient-Gesellschaft 97. Saarbrücken: Saarbrücker Druckerei und Verlag.

Damati, E., and Stepanski, Y.

1996   A Middle Bronze Age Burial Cave on Mt. Canaan, Zefat. *'Atiqot* 29: 1–29, 107–8.

de Feyter, T.

1988   The Metal Finds. Pp. 609–26 in *Hammam et-Turkman I: Report on the University of Amsterdam's 1981–84 Excavations in Syria*, ed. M. van Loon. Istanbul: Nederlands Historisch-Archeologisch Instituut.

Dever, W. G.

1975   Middle Bronze Age IIA Cemeteries at 'Ain Es-Samiyeh and Sinjil. *Bulletin of the American Schools of Oriental Research* 217: 23–26.

1987   Funerary Practices in EB IV (MB I) Palestine: A Study in Cultural Discontinuity. Pp. 9–19 in *Love and Death in the Ancient Near East*, eds. J. Marks and R. Good. Guilford, CT: Four Quarters.

1992   Pastorialism and the End of the Urban Early Bronze Age in Palestine. Pp. 83–92 in *Pastoralism in the Levant: Archaeological Materials in Anthropological Perspectives*, eds. O. Bar-Yosef and A. Khazanov. Monographs in World Archaeology 10. Madison, WI: Prehistory.

Dothan, M.

1956   The Sacrifical Mound at Nahariya. *Eretz Israel* 4: 41–46.

Doumet-Serhal, C.

2001   Third Season of Excavation at Sidon. Preliminary Report. *Baal* 5: 153–72.

2002   Fourth Season of Excavation at Sidon. Preliminary Report. *Baal* 6: 179–210.

du Mesnil du Buisson, R.

1948   *Baghouz – L'ancienne Corsôtê: Le tell archaïque et la nécropole de l'Age du Bronze.* Documenta et Monumenta Orientis Antiqui 3. Leiden: Brill.

Dunand, M.

1939   *Fouilles de Byblos I, 1926–1932.* Paris: Geuthner.

1950   *Fouilles de Byblos 1933–38,* Vol. 2. Paris: Geuthner.

1954   *Fouilles de Byblos II,* Part I. Paris: Geuthner.

Eisenberg, E.

1985   A Burial Cave of the Early Middle Bronze Age IV (MB I) near 'Enan. *'Atiqot* 17: 59–74.

1993   Kitan, Tel. Pp. 878–91 in *The New Encyclopedia of Archaeological Excavations in the Holy Land*, ed. E. Stern. Jerusalem: Israel Exploration Society.

El-Amin, M., and Mallowan, M. E. L.

1950   Soundings in the Makhmur Plain. *Sumer* 5: 55–68.

Engberg, R. M.

1942   Tombs of the Early Second Millennium from Baghuz on the Middle Euphrates. *Bulletin of the American Schools of Oriental Research* 87: 17–23.

Epstein, C.

1974   Middle Bronze Age Tombs at Kefar Szold and Ginosar. *'Atiqot* 7: 13–39 (Hebrew).

1985   Dolmens Excavated in the Golan. *'Atiqot* 17: 2–58.

Epstein C., and Guttman, S.

1972   The Golan Survery. Pp. 243–98 in *Judea, Samaria and the Golan: Archaeological Survey, 1967–1968*, ed. M. Kochavi. Jerusalem: Archaeological Survey of Israel (Hebrew).

Falconer, S. E.

1985   Village Pottery Production and Exchange: a Jordan Valley Perspective. Pp. 251–59 in *Studies in the History and Archaeology of Jordan 3*, ed. A. Hadidi. Amman: Department of Antiquities.

1995   Rural Response to Early Urbanism: Bronze Age Household and Village Economy at Tell el-Hayyat, Jordan. *Journal of Field Archaeology* 22: 399–419.

Falconer, S. E., and Magness-Gardiner, B.

1984   Preliminary Report of the First Season of the Tell el-Hayyat Project. *Bulletin of the American Schools of Oriental Research* 255: 49–74.

Faust, A.

2005   The Canaanite Village: Social Structure of Middle Bronze Age Rural Communities. *Levant* 37: 105–25.

Ferembach, D.; Furshpan, A; and Perrot, J.

1975   Une sépulture collective du Bronze Moyen à Kh. Minha (Munhata), Israel. Pp. 87–117 in *Report on Archaeological Work at Suwwanet eth Thaniya and Khirbet Minha (Munhata)*, ed. G. Landes. Bulletin of the American Schools of Oriental Research Supplement 21. Missoula, MT: Scholars.

Garfinkel, Y.

1988   Gesher. *Excavations and Surveys in Israel* 6: 54–55.

1990a Gesher (Neve Ur) – 1987. *Excavations and Surveys in Israel* 7–8: 62–63.

1990b Excavations at Gesher – A Pre-Pottery A Neolithic Site and a Middle Bronze Age IIa Cemetery. *Qadmoniot* 89–90: 26–31 (Hebrew).

1993   Gesher. Pp. 492–93 in *The New Encyclopedia of Archaeological Excavations in the Holy Land*, ed. F. Stern. Jerusalem: Israel Exploration Society.

2001   Warrior Burial Customs in the Levant during the Early Second Millennium B.C. Pp. 143–61 in *Studies in the Archaeology of*

Israel and Neighboring Lands in Memory of Douglas L. Esse, ed. S. Wolff. Studies in Ancient Oriental Civilization 59. Chicago, IL: Oriental Institute.

Garfinkel, Y., and Bonfil, R.

1990   Graves and Burial Customs of the MBIIa Period in Gesher. Eretz *Israel* 21: 106, 132–47 (Hebrew with English summary).

Garfinkel, Y., and Dag, D.

2006   *Gesher: A Pre-Pottery Neolithic A Site in the Central Jordan Valley, Israel. A Final Report.* Berlin: Ex Oriente.

Garfinkel Y., and Nadel, D.

1989   The Sultanian Flint Assemblage from Gesher and its Implications for Recognizing early Neolithic Entities in the Levant. *Paléorient* 15, no. 2: 139–51.

Gates, M.-H.

1988   Dialogues Between Ancient Near Eastern Texts and the Archaeological Record: Test Cases from Bronze Age Syria. *Bulletin of the American Schools of Oriental Research* 270: 63–91.

Gershuny, L.

1989   Tomb 990. Pp. 14–19 in *Excavations at Kabri, Preliminary Report of the 1988 Season*, ed. A. Kempinski. Tel Aviv: Tel Aviv University (Hebrew).

Gerstenblith, P.

1980   A Reassessment of the Beginning of the Middle Bronze Age in Syria-Palestine. *Bulletin of the American Schools of Oriental Research* 237: 65–84.

1983   *The Levant at the Beginning of the Middle Bronze Age.* American Schools of Oriental Research Dissertation Series 5. Winona Lake, IN: Eisenbrauns.

Gibson, M.

1988–89   Nippur. *The Oriental Institute Annual Report:* 9–17.

Gonen, R. (ed.)

2001   *Excavations at Efrata. A Burial Ground from the Intermediate and Middle Bronze Ages.* Israel Antiquities Authority Reports 12. Jerusalem: Israel Antiquities Authority.

Gophna, R.

1979   A Middle Bronze Age II Village in the Jordan Valley. *Tel Aviv* 6: 28–33.

Gophna, R., and Sussman, V.

1969   A Middle Bronze Age Tomb at Barqai. *'Atiqot* 5: 1–13 (Hebrew).

Griffith, F. L.

1890   *The Antiquities of Tell el Yahūdīyeh and Miscellaneous Work in Egypt During the Years 1887–1888.* Seventh Memoir. London: Egypt Exploration Society.

1926   A Drinking Syphon from Tell el-'Amarnah. *Journal of Egyptian Archaeology* 12: 22–23.

Grigson, C.

1995   Plough and Pasture in the Early Economy of the Southern Levant. Pp. 245–68 in *The Archaeology of Society in the Holy Land,* ed. T. Levy. London: Leicester University.

Grosvenor Ellis, A., and Westley, B.

1965   Appendix J: Preliminary Report on the Animal Remains in the Jericho Tombs, and Appendix K (i): Observations on the Occurrence of Animal Bones in the EB–MB Tombs. Pp. 694–703 in *Excavations at Jericho II,* ed. K. M. Kenyon, London: British School of Archaeology in Jerusalem.

Guigues, P. E.

1937   Lébé'a, Kafer-Garra, Qrayé, nécropoles de la région sidonienne. *Bulletin du Musée de Beyrouth* 1: 35–76.

1938   Lébé'a, Kafer-Garra, Qrayé, nécropoles de la région sidonienne. *Bulletin du Musée de Beyrouth* 2: 27–72.

Guy, P. L. O.

1938   *Megiddo Tombs.* University of Chicago Oriental Institute Publications 33. Chicago, IL: University of Chicago.

Hallote, R.

1994   Mortuary Practices and their Implications for Social Organization in the Middle Bronze Southern Levant. Unpublished Ph.D. dissertation, University of Chicago.

1995   Mortuary Archaeology and the Middle Bronze Age Southern Levant. *Journal of Mediterranean Archaeology* 8: 93–122.

Hartman, L. F., and Oppenheim, A. L.

1950   *On Beer and Brewing Techniques in Ancient Mesopotamia.* Supplement to the Journal of the American Oriental Society 10. Baltimore: American Oriental Society.

Henschel-Simon, E.

1938   The 'Toggle-Pins' in the Palestine Archaeological Museum. *Quarterly of the Department of Antiquities of Palestine* 6: 169–209.

Hess, O.

1990   Finds from a Cemetery in Nahal Tavor. *'Atiqot* 10: 157–59, 36 (Hebrew).

Hesse, B., and Wapnish, P.

1981   Animal Remains from the Bab edh-Dhra Cemetery. Pp. 133–36 in *The Southeastern Dead Sea Plain Expedition, An Interim Report of the 1977 Season,* eds. W. E. Rast and R. T. Schaub. Annual of the American Schools of Oriental Research 46. Cambridge, MA: American Schools of Oriental Research.

Homan, M.

2004   Beer and Its Drinkers: An Ancient Near Eastern Love Story. *Near Eastern Archaeology* 67 no. 2: 84–95.

Hopf, M.

1983 Appendix B: Jericho Plant Remains. Pp. 576–621 in *Excavations at Jericho V: The Pottery Phases of the Tell and Other Finds,* eds. K. M. Kenyon and T. A. Holland. London: British School of Archaeology in Jerusalem.

Horwitz, L. K.

1987 Animal Offerings from Two Middle Bronze Age Tombs. *Israel Exploration Journal* 37: 251–55.

1989 Diachronic Changes in Rural Husbandry Practices in Bronze Age Settlements from the Refaim Valley, Israel. *Palestine Exploration Quarterly* 121: 44–54.

1996a Animal Bones from the Middle Bronze Age Tombs at Tel Dan. Pp. 268–77 in *Dan I: A Chronicle of the Excavations, the Pottery Neolithic, the Early Bronze Age, and the Middle Bronze Age Tombs,* eds. A. Biran, D. Ilan and R. Greenberg. Jerusalem: Nelson Glueck School of Biblical Archaeology.

1996b Fauna from Tel Sasa, 1980. *'Atiqot* 28: 59–61.

1997 The Animal Bone Assemblage from the Middle Bronze II Tomb (T1181, Area L) at Hazor. Pp. 344–47 in *Hazor V: An Account of the Fifth Season of Excavation, 1968,* eds. Y. Yadin and A. Ben-Tor. Jerusalem: Israel Exploration Society.

2001a Animal Offerings in the Middle Bronze Age: Food for the Gods, Food for Thought. *Palestine Exploration Quarterly* 133: 78–90.

2001b Animal Remains from Efrata. Pp. 110–18 in *Excavations at Efrata: A Burial Ground from the Intermediate and Middle Bronze Ages,* ed. R. Gonen. Israel Antiquities Authority Reports 12. Jerusalem: Israel Antiquities Authority.

Horwitz, L. K., and Garfinkel, Y.

1991 Animal Remains from the Site of Gesher, Central Jordan Valley. *Mitekufat Haeven (Journal of the Israel Prehistoric Society)* 24: 64–76.

Horwitz, L. K.; Bar Giora, N.; Mienis, H. K.; and Lernau, O.

2005 Faunal and Malacological Remains from the Middle Bronze, Late Bronze and Iron Age Levels at Tel Yoqneam. Pp. 395–435 in *Yoqneam III: The Middle and Late Bronze Ages. Final Report of the Archaeological Excavations (1977–1988),* eds. A. Ben-Tor, D. Ben-Ami and A. Livneh. Qedem Reports 7. Jerusalem: Institute of Archaeology.

Hrouda, B.

1990 Die Altbabylonischen Tumuli von Baghūz dei Mâri: Begräbnisse der Hanäer? Pp. 103–14 in *De la Babylonie à la Syrie, en passant par Mari. Mélanges offerts à Monsieur J.-R. Kupper à l'occasion de son 70e anniversaire,* ed. Ö. Tunca. Liège: Université de Liège.

Ikram, S.

2001 Diet. Pp. 390–95 in *The Oxford Encyclopedia of Ancient Egypt,* Vol. 1, ed. D. B. Redford. Oxford: Oxford University.

Ilan, D.

1992 A Middle Bronze Age Cache from Tel Dan. *Eretz Israel* 23: 9–20 (Hebrew).

1995 Mortuary Practices at Tel Dan in the Middle Bronze Age: a Reflection of Canaanite Society and Ideology. Pp. 117–39 in *The Archaeology of Death in the Ancient Near East,* eds. S. Campbell and A. Green. Oxford: Oxbow.

1996 The Middle Bronze Age Tombs. Pp. 161–328 in *Dan I: A Chronicle of the Excavations, the Pottery Neolithic, the Early Bronze Age, and the Middle Bronze Age Tombs,* eds. A. Biran, D. Ilan and R. Greenberg. Jerusalem: Nelson Glueck School of Biblical Archaeology.

Kan-Cipor-Meron, T.

2003 Middle Bronze Age Metal Objects from the Rishon Le-Zion Cemetery. Unpublished M.A. Thesis, University of Haifa.

Kantor, H.

1978 Chogha Mish and Chogha Bonut. *The Ori-*
-79 *ental Institute Annual Report 1978–79:*
33–9.

Kaplan, Y.

1959 *The Archaeology and History of Tel-Aviv
– Jaffa.* Ramat Gan: Massada.

Karmon, Y.

1971 *Israel: A Regional Geography.* New York:
Wiley Interscience.

Kempinski, A.

2002 *Tel Kabri: The 1986–1993 Excavation Seasons.*
Institute of Archaeology, Tel Aviv University, Monograph Series 20. Tel Aviv: Yass.

Kempinski, A.; Gershuny, L.;
and Scheftelowitz, N.

2002 Pottery: III. Middle Bronze Age. Pp. 109–75
in *Tel Kabri: The 1986–1993 Excavation
Seasons.* Institute of Archaeology, Tel Aviv
University, Monograph Series 20. Tel Aviv:
Yass.

Kenyon, K. M.

1960 *Excavations at Jericho, Vol. I: The Tombs Excavated in 1952–54.* London: British School
of Archaeology in Jerusalem.

1965 *Excavations at Jericho, Vol. II: The Tombs Excavated in 1955–58.* London: British School
of Archaeology in Jerusalem.

Khalil, L.

1980 The Composition and Technology of Ancient Copper Alloy Artifacts from Jericho
and Related Sites. Unpublished Ph.D. Thesis, Institute of Archaeology, University of
London.

Kishon, V., and Hellwing, S.

1990 Animal Bones from Tell Kabri: Area D
Middle Bronze. Pp. 47–50 in *Excavations at
Kabri: Preliminary Report of the 1989 Season
4,* eds. A. Kempinski and W. D. Niemeier.
Tel Aviv: Tel Aviv University.

Kislev, M.; Artzy, M.; and Marcus, E.

1993 Import of an Aegean Food Plant to a Middle
Bronze IIA Coastal Site in Israel. *Levant* 25:
145–54.

Kochavi, M.; Beck, P.; and Gophna, R.

1979 Aphek-Antipatris, Tel Poleg, Tel Zeror, and
Tel Burga: Four Fortified Sites of the Middle
Bronze IIA in the Sharon Plain. *Zeitschrift
des Deutschen Palästina-Vereins* 95: 121–65.

Kochavi, M., and Yadin, E.

2002 Typological Analysis of the MB IIA Pottery
from Aphek According to its Stratigraphic
Provenance. Pp. 189–225 in *The Middle
Bronze Age in the Levant. Proceedings of an
International Conference on MB IIA Ceramic
Material, Vienna, 24th–26th of January,
2001,* ed. M. Bietak. Wien: Österreichische
Akademie der Wissenschaften.

Lapp, P.

1966 *The Dhahr Mirzbaneh Tombs.* New Haven, CT:
American Schools of Oriental Research.

Loud, G.

1948 *Megiddo II: Seasons of 1935–39.* Oriental
Institute Publications 62. Chicago, IL: University of Chicago.

Macalister, R. A. S.

1912 *The Excavation of Gezer, 1902–1905 and
1907–1909,* Vols. I–III. London: Murray.

Maeir, A.

1997a The Material Culture of the Central Jordan
Valley during the Middle Bronze II Period:
Pottery and Settlement Pattern. Vols. I and
II. Unpublished Ph.D. Dissertation, Institute
of Archaeology, The Hebrew University in
Jerusalem.

1997b Tomb 1181: A Multiple-Interment Burial
Cave of the Transitional Middle Bronze Age
IIA–B. Pp. 295–340 in *Hazor V: An Account
of the Fifth Season of Excavation, 1968,* eds.
Y. Yadin and A. Ben-Tor. Jerusalem: Israel
Exploration Society.

2002   Perspectives on the Early MB II Period in the Jordan Valley. Pp. 261–67 in *The Middle Bronze Age in the Levant. Proceedings of an International Conference on MB IIA Ceramic Material, Vienna, 24th–26th of January, 2001,* ed. M. Bietak. Wien: Österreichische Akademie der Wissenschaften.

Maeir, A., and Garfinkel, Y.

1992   Bone and Metal Straw-tip Beer-Strainers from the Ancient Near East. *Levant* 24: 218–23.

Magueron, J.-C.

1975   Quatre campagnes de fouilles à Emar 1972–1974: Un bilan provisoire. *Syria* 52: 53–85.

Maisler, B.

1939   Tell Kurdane (Aphek?) in the Plain of Acre. *Bulletin of the Jewish Exploration Society* 6: 151–58 (Hebrew).

Mallowan, M. E. L.

1936   The Excavations at Tall Chagar Bazar, and an Archaeological Survey of the Habur Region, 1934–45. Iraq 3: 1–86.

1937   The Excavations at Tall Chagar Bazar, and an Archaeological Survey of the Habur Region, Second Season, 1936. Iraq 4: 91–177.

Maxwell-Hyslop, R.

1949   Western Asiatic Shaft-Hole Axes. *Iraq* 11: 90–129.

Meyer, J.-W., and Pruss, A.

1994   Ausgrabungen in Halawa 2: Die Kleinfunde von Tell Halawa A. Schriften Zur Vorderasiatischen Archäologie 6. Saarbrücken: Saarbrücker Druckerei und Verlag.

Miron, E.

1992   *Axes and Adzes from Canaan.* Prähistorische Bronzefunde IX, 19. Stuttgart: Steiner.

Moorey, P. R. S.

1980   Metal Wine Sets in the Ancient Near East. *Iranica Antiqua* 15: 181–97.

Murray, M. A.

2000   Fruits, Vegetables, Pulses and Condiments. Pp. 609–55 in *Ancient Egyptian Materials and Technology,* eds. P. T. Nicholson and I. Shaw. Cambridge: Cambridge University.

Newberry, P. E.

1893   *Beni Hasan I.* London: Kegan Paul, Trench, Trübner.

Northover, P.

1989   Properties and Use of Arsenic-Copper Alloys. Pp. 113–18 in *Old World Archaeometallurgy,* eds. A. Hauptmann, E. Pernicka and G. A. Wagner. Bochum: Deutsches Bergbau-Museum.

Oren, E.

1971   A Middle Bronze Age I Warrior Tomb at Beth-Shan. *Zeitschrift des Deutschen Palästina-Vereins* 87: 109–39.

1973   *The Northern Cemetery of Beth Shan.* Leiden: Brill.

Ory, J.

1938   Excavations at Ras el-'Ain. *Quarterly of the Department of Antiquities of Palestine* 6: 99–120.

1948   A Bronze-Age Cemetery at Dhahrat el Humraiya. *Quarterly of the Department of Antiquities of Palestine* 13: 75–89.

Paley, S. M., and Porath, Y.

1997   Early Middle Bronze Age IIa Remains at Tel el-Ifshar, Israel: A Preliminary Report. Pp. 369–78 in *The Hyksos: New Historical and Archaeological Perspectives,* ed. E. Oren. Philadelphia, PA: Pennsylvania University Museum.

Parker, B.

1949   Cylinder Seals from Palestine. *Iraq* 11: 1–43.

Parrot, A.

1962   Les Fouilles de Mari. Douzième campagne (Automne 1961). *Syria* 39: 151–79.

Pearce, J., and Luff, R.

1994 The Taphonomy of Cooked Bone. Pp. 51–56 in *Whither Environmental Archaeology?*, eds. R. Luff and P. Rowley-Conwy. Oxbow Monograph 38. Oxford: Oxbow.

Petrie, W. M. F.

1917 *Tools and Weapons.* British School of Archaeology in Egypt and Egyptian Research Account Twenty Second Year, 1916. London: British School of Archaeology in Egypt.

1932 *Ancient Gaza II: Tell el Ajjul.* London: British School of Archaeology in Egypt.

1934 *Ancient Gaza IV: Tell el Ajjul.* London: British School of Archaeology in Egypt.

1937 *Anthedon.* London: Quaritch.

Petrie, W. M. F.; Mackay, E. J. H.; and Murray, M. A.

1952 *City of the Shepherd Kings and Ancient Gaza V.* London: British School of Archaeology in Egypt.

Philip, G.

1989 *Metal Weapons of the Early and Middle Bronze Ages in Syria-Palestine.* Parts 1 and 2. British Archaeological Reports International Series 526. Oxford: British Archaeological Reports

1991 Tin, Arsenic, Lead: Alloying Practices in Syria-Palestine around 2000 BC. *Levant* 23: 93–104.

1995a Tell El-Dab'a Metalwork, Patterns and Purpose. Pp. 66–83 in *Egypt, the Aegean and the Levant: Interconnections in the Second Millennium BC,* eds. W. V. Davies and L. Schofield. London: British Museum.

1995b Warrior Burials in the Ancient Near-Eastern Bronze Age: The Evidence from Mesopotamia, Western Iran and Syria-Palestine. Pp. 140–54 in *The Archaeology of Death in the Ancient Near East,* eds.S. Campbell and A. Green. Oxford: Oxbow.

1997 The Metal Objects. Pp. 113–24 in *Excavations at Tell Brak 1: The Mitanni and Old Babylonian Periods,* eds. D. Oates, J. Oates, and H. McDonald. McDonald Institute Monographs. Cambridge: British School of Archaeology in Iraq.

Piontek, J.

1999 *Biologia populacji pradziejowych.* Poznań: Wydawnictwo Naukowe.

Prag, K.

1974 The Intermediate Early Bronze–Middle Bronze: An Interpretation of the Evidence from Transjordan, Syria and Lebanon. *Levant* 6: 69–116.

Price-Williams, D.

1977 *The Tombs of the Middle Bronze Age IIA Period from the '500' Cemetery at Tell el-Far'a (South).* Institute of Archaeology Occasional Publication 1. London: Institute of Archaeology.

Pritchard, J.

1963 *The Bronze Age Cemetery at Gibeon.* Philadephia, PA: Pennsylvania University Museum.

Prummel, W., and Frisch, H.

1986 A Guide for the Distinction of Species, Sex and Body Side in Bones of Sheep and Goat. *Journal of Archaeological Science* 13: 567–77.

Radwan, A.

1983 *Die Kupfer- und Bronzegefäße Ägyptens (Von den Anfängen bis zum Beginn der Spätzeit).* Prähistorische Bronzefunde II/2. Munich: Beck.

Rosenfeld, A.; Ilani, S.; and Dvorachek, M.

1997 Bronze Alloys from Canaan during the Middle Bronze Age. *Journal of Archaeological Science* 24: 857–64.

Salonen, E.

1965 *Die Hausgeräte der Alten Mesopotamier, I.* Annales Academiae Scientiarum Fennicae Ser B. 1 139. Helsinki: Societas Orientalis Fennica.

Sass, B.

2004 Pre-Bronze Age and Bronze Age Artifacts. Pp. 1450–1524 in *The Renewed Archaeological Excavations at Lachish (1973–1994)*, Vol. III, ed. D. Ussishkin. Institute of Archaeology, Tel Aviv University, Monograph Series 22. Tel Aviv: Yass.

Schaeffer, C. F. A

1949 *Ugaritica II*. Paris: Geuthner.
1962 *Ugaritica IV*. Paris: Geuthner.

Scheftelowitz, N., and Gershuny, L.

2002 The Middle Bronze Age. Pp. 29–34 in *Tel Kabri: The 1986–1993 Excavation Seasons*. Institute of Archaeology, Tel Aviv University, Monograph Series 20. Tel Aviv: Yass.

Schmidt, K.

2002 *Norşuntepe: Kleinfunde II. Artifakte aus Felsgestein, Knochen und Geweih, Ton, Metall und Glas*. Mainz: Zabern.

Shalev, S.

1996 Archaeometallurgy in Israel: The Impact of the Material on the Choice of Shape, Size and Colour of Ancient Products. Pp. 11–15 in *Archaeometry 94: The Proceedings of the 29th International Symposium on Archaeometry*, eds. S. Demirci, A. M. Özer and O. Summers. Ankara: Tübitak.
2000 Metal Artifacts: Archaeometallurgy. Pp. 278–87 in *Aphek-Antipatris I. Excavation of Areas A and B: The 1972–1976 Seasons*, eds. M. Kochavi, P. Beck, P. and E. Yadin. Institute of Archaeology, Tel Aviv University, Monograph Series 19. Tel Aviv: Yass.
2002 Metal Artifacts: Middle Bronze Age II. Pp. 307–18 in *Tel Kabri: The 1986–1993 Excavation Seasons*. Institute of Archaeology, Tel Aviv University, Monograph Series 20. Tel Aviv: Yass.

Shenberg, C.

1985 Analysis of the Weapons by X-ray Fluorescence Method. *'Atiqot* 17: 112.

Silver, I. A.

1969 The Ageing of Domestic Animals. Pp. 283–302 in *Science in Archaeology*, eds. D. Brothwell and E. S. Higgs. London: Thames and Hudson.

Simon, C.

1992 Râpes, siphons ou filtres pour pailles: développement égyptien d'un art de boire. Pp. 555–63 in *Atti del VI Congresso Internazionale di Egittologia, Torino*, Vol. 1. Turin: Comitato Organizzativo del Congresso.

Smith, R. H.

1962 *Excavations in the Cemetery at Khirbet Kufin, Palestine*. London: Quaritch.

Sparks, R. T.

2004 Canaan in Egypt: Archaeological Evidence for a Social Phenomenon. Pp. 25–54 in *Invention and Innovation: The Social Context of Technological Change, 2: Egypt, the Aegean and the Near East, 1650–1150 BC*, eds. J. Bourriau and J. Philips. Oxford: Oxbow.

Sukenik, E. L.

1948 Archaeological Excavations at 'Affula. *Journal of the Palestine Oriental Society* 21: 1–79.

Sussman, V.

1966 Middle Bronze Age Burials at Moza. *'Atiqot* 3: 5 (Hebrew).

Thomas, A. P.

1981 *Gurob: A New Kingdom Town. Introduction and Catalogue of Objects in the Petrie Collection*. Warminster: Aris and Phillips.

Thrane, H.

1978 *Sukas IV: A Middle Bronze Age Collective Grave on Tall Sukas*. Copenhagen: Munksgaard.

Tpilinsky, N.

1962 Meron. *Hadashot Archeologiyot* 2: 25 (Hebrew).

Tubb, J. N.

1983   The MBIIA Period in Palestine: Its Relation-
        ship with Syria and Its Origin. *Levant* 15:
        49–62.

1985   Some Observations on Spearheads in Pales-
        tine in the Middle and Late Bronze Ages. Pp.
        189–96 in *Palestine in the Bronze and Iron
        Ages. Papers on Honour of Olga Tufnell*, ed.
        J. N. Tubb. London: Institute of Archaeol-
        ogy.

Tufnell, O.

1958   *Lachish IV: The Bronze Age.* London: Oxford
        University.

1962   The Courtyard Cemetery at Tell el-'Ajjul,
        Palestine. *Bulletin of the Institute of Archae-
        ology* 3: 1–37.

Tufnell, O., and Ward, W.

1966   Relations between Byblos, Egypt and Meso-
        potamia at the End of the Third Millennium
        BC. A Study of the Montet Jar. *Syria* 43:
        165–241.

Tzori, N.

1962   An Archaeological Survey in the Beth-
        Shean Valley. Pp. 135–98 in *The Beth-Shean
        Valley* (The 17th Archaeological Conven-
        tion). Jerusalem: Central (Hebrew).

Ussishkin, D.

2004   *The Renewed Archaeological Excavations at
        Lachish (1973–1994).* Institute of Archaeol-
        ogy, Tel Aviv University, Monograph Series
        22. Tel Aviv: Yass.

Vandier d'Abbadie, J.

1937   *Catalogue des ostraca figurés de Deir el Mé-
        dineh.* Documents de Fouilles de l'Institut
        Français d'Archeologie Orientale du Caire
        2,2. Cairo: Institut Français d'Archeologie
        Orientale du Caire.

Vincent, L.-H.

1947   Une grotte funéraire dans Ouady et-Tin.
        Revue Biblique 54: 269–82.

Werner, P.

1998   *Tall Munbaqa – Bronzezeit in Syrien.* Neu-
        münster: Wachholtz.

Woolley, C. L.

1955   *Alalakh.* London: Society of Antiquaries.

Yadin, Y.

1963   *The Art of Warfare in Biblical Lands.* Lon-
        don: Weidenfeld and Nicolson.

Yogev, O.

1985   A Middle Bronze Age Cemetery South of
        Tel Rehov. *'Atiqot* 17: 90–110.

Ziffer, I.

1990   *At That Time the Canaanites Were in the
        Land: Daily Life in Canaan in the Middle
        Bronze Age 2, 2000–1550 BCE.* Exhibition
        catalogue. Tel Aviv: Eretz Israel Museum.

Zohary, M.

1972   *Flora Palaestina,* Vol. II. Jerusalem: Israel
        Academy of Sciences and Humanities.

Contributors

Ruhama Bonfil
Institute of Archaeology
The Hebrew University of Jerusalem

Susan Cohen
Montana State University
Department of History and Philosophy

Yosef Garfinkel
Institute of Archaeology
The Hebrew University of Jerusalem

Orna Hess
Israel Antiquities Authority

Liora Kolska Horwitz
Department of Evolution,
Systematics and Ecology
The Hebrew University of Jerusalem

Nili Liphschitz
Head, Botanical Laboratory
Institute of Archaeology
Tel Aviv University

Aren M. Maeir
The Institute of Archaeology
The Martin (Szusz) Department of
Land of Israel Studies and Archaeology
Bar-Ilan University

Sariel Shalev
University of Haifa &
Weizmann Institute of Science

Wieslaw Więckowski
Department of Historical Anthropology
Institute of Archaeology
University of Warsaw